AF333014

BEAUTY and WISDOM
OF
THE HOLY QURAN

By

Abdul Karim Chippa

KITAB BHAVAN
New Delhi-110002

KITAB BHAVAN
Exporters & Importers
1784, Kalan Mahal, Daryaganj
New Delhi- 110002. (India)
Phones: 3274686, 263383
Telex No. 31-63106 ALI IN

First Published in India 1979
4th. Edition   .. 1990

ISBN 81-7151-027-2

Published by:
Nusrat Ali Nasri for Kitab Bhavan
1784, Kalan Mahal, Daryaganj
New Delhi- 110002

Printed in India :
at Lahoti Fine Art Press
1711, Sui Walan
New Delhi-110002

CONTENTS

		PAGE.
1.	Introduction	VII
2.	Preface. To the 1st & 4th Editions	IX–X
3.	Conception of God.	1
4.	Prayers and their usefulness	21
	(a) Meanings of Surah-i-Fateha (the opening chapter).	34
	(b) Quranic Prayers.	39
5.	Science and the Holy Quran—	
	(i) Origin of the Universe.	41
	(ii) Evolution of Man.	43
	(iii) Holy Quran's emphasis on the study of Sciences.	45
	(iv) Significance of Surah-i-Rehman.	51
	(v) Mysteries of life.	56
	(vi) Significance of Surah-i-Yusuf.	58
	(vii) Beauty of the Holy Quran.	62
	(a) Significance of Surah-i-Noor	69
	(b) Mysticism of Imam Ghazali.	74

6. The rarest gems of intellectual beauty.
   (Quotations from the Holy Quran.)   ..   79

7. Importance of the Science of Hadith—
   The glittering gems of wisdom   98

   (a) Extracts from the speeches of the Holy
       Prophet.   108

   (b) A few famous sayings of the Holy Prophet. ..   112

8. The cosmics Hazrads of the Planet Earth ..   119

   Bibliography   127

INTRODUCTION

The writer of this small book Mr. Abdul Karim Chippa, B.A., LL.B. (Alig). is a very recent acquaintance of mine. But the more I come to know him the more I am impressed by his learning, his obvious sincerity and simplicity and his deep faith. His failing eyesight has not proved to be an obstacle to his insight in matters of religion nor to his efforts to convey to his younger brothers in faith the beauty and wisdom of the Holy Quran.

In very simple language he has expressed his idea of the essentially dynamic teachings of Islam with special reference to modern conceptions of life inspired by the advances in science, technology, sociology and rational philosophy.

Islam is the most secular of all religions inasmuch as man's life in this world is stated therein to be a prelude to the life hereafter. As you sow, so shall you reap, it says. It in essence teaches what is right and what is wrong in human affairs. It defines individual rights and strikes a happy balance between individual and collective rights and liabilities. Having done this it leaves to each age to choose its own form of government and state.

For the inner life of a man it preaches piety with the only sanction of Fear of God which one has to cultivate. And once this is done no more powerful sanction is needed in life.

Mr. Chippa who has also gone into the question of a modern tendency to be-little Hadith. The controversy requires deep thought and understanding. But one has to agree that Mr. Chippa has taken the right view of the matter.

He has given a good bibliography. As an individual effort the book deserves all praise and should be welcomed by all students of religion specially those who think that modern scientific and Philosophic advances have obviated the necessity of religion altogether.

Sd. MEHDI ALI SIDDIQUI,
M.A., LL.B. (Alig.),
(Add. Sessions Judge, Karachi.)

PREFACE

This is an humble attempt on our part to bring into prominence the central scriptural truth of the Holy Quran, the divine message, which establishes true relationship between man and man, and his universe, and between man and his Creator. We have no claim to any scholarship, nor to any authority on the subject of the knowledge of the Holy Quran. But this is our first attempt due to inner promptings, this book, therefore, suffers from immaturities. We have done as far as possible for us to put forth in the simplest manner the Quranic Conception of God and its importance for the formation of a pure faith in this age of doubt and scepticism.

We learn that there are plans afoot to undervalue and to be-little the importance of the Science of Hadith, which is indispensable for the understanding of the Holy Book. We therefore, deprecate such attempts, if any, in any quarter; to attack and assail the knowledge of the traditions available to us, is to attack the very base of the Holy Quran, the divinity and miraculousness of which has been attested to by men of faith, piety, and by persons possessing incorruptibility.

The Islamic World in general is face to face with cultural and ideological challenges from the West and specially from the Eastern Paganistic world, where marxims, a new religion, is having its way and occupying the vacuum created through the decay of true religion, morality, and spiritual values. The remedy lies in the acquiring of technological knowledge for the development of industry and for other purposes as well, and in the removal of ignorance and poverty; secondly, the remedy lies in the revival of true faith and its institutions of Salat and Zakat in letter and spirit. (It must be mentioned that the present revolutionary government of Pakistan is doing its utmost to secure these ends and is moving with the times

It must be added that the Holy Quran calls the true believers as "The Nation of the Middle Path", which implies that the Muslims are neither Communists, nor capitalists, nor paganists, but members of an International Society (Millat) treading the golden middle path, occupying the centre or the heart of the globe. If we, who call ourselves as Muslims, hold fast to the moorings of the Holy Quran and follow the precept of the Holy Prophet (peace be on Him), we can successfully meet any challenge, however, formidable it may be from any quarter.

The Holy Quran declares God's mercy and His grace for the true believers. "Allah hath promised such of you as believe and do good works that He will surely make them to succeed (the present rulers) in the earth even as He caused those who were before them to succeed (others); and that He will surely establish for them their religion which He hath approved for them, and will give them in exchange safety after their fear. They serve Me. They ascribe nothing as partner unto Me. Those who disbelieve henceforth, they are the miscreants.

"Establish worship and pay the poor-due and obey the messenger, that haply ye may find mercy". Quran (Surah-i-Noor), Light.

x

It is, therefore, the sacred task of the present day intellectuals to expound the Quranic ideology to counter the ideological war being waged by the East or the West.

Lastly, we thank all the authors whom we have quoted in this book. We are specially indebted to Allama Yusuf Ali and Mohammad Pikhtall for quoting from their English translations of the Holy Book.

We are also indebted to Mr. Mehdi Ali Siddiqi for his kind introduction to our endeavour and for his keen interest in the literary efforts, despite his onerous duties as an Additional Session's Judge, Karachi.

Abdul Karim Chippa,
Karachi.

Jan 1962

PREFACE TO THE 4th EDITION

—:o:—

Sciences' spectacular giant strides towards the unlocking of the mysteries of God's wonderous creations are singular and very astonishing. Equally sciences' efforts to ease the burden of human drudgery and labours through automatic devices and through sophisticated appliances are praiseworthy and creditable. Also, the thrust of men bearing space crafts and rockets towards the moon, and lunar landings of the spacecrafts on the crater-laden moon itself are breathtaking. There is a universal acknowledgement and acclaimation for the varied and spectacular feats of science in the material spheres of human ingenuity and knowledge and for the heaps of benefits conferred in the form of ease and comforts on man. In short, our modern knowledge has done much in the removal of numerous bottlenecks in the ways of humanitys' understanding of the secrets of nature.

But it must be said that despite our immense advances in the sphere of sciences, we have failed to kill the dangerous virus of Godlessness which is eating into the very vitals of our spiritual self. The more we have progressed in the sciences and technology and through it in the attainment of bodily ease and comfort, the deeper we are sinking in the morass of spiritual and moral degradation, and to day there exists on a global scale the worst diseases of the mind, body, and of the soul. We have begun to believe wrongly that the universe exists eternally only for baser puposes and that our life has no divine goals. The speculations, however, of the men of sciences about the Sun, the life-giver of our globe are noteworthy David Bergamani and his colleauges write in the 'Universe', a highly illustrated, and creditable book.

(P. 24), "It (Sun) was born out of cloud of gas some 5000 million years ago, and quickly assumed the characteristics it has to day. The suns' present age of 5000 millions years of normal life, have passed, and another 5000 millions lie ahead". " If the sun could continue to spend only 584 million tons of hydrogen per second, it will go on burning for another 50,000 millions of years or more, in about 5000 millions the quickening will set in and the sun will start swelling and over an space of about a thousand millions years, the average temperature on earth will rise to something like 500 C, and unless some super human race shows extra-ordinary forethought, and devises marvellous shielding, oceans will boil away, lead will melt like molasses and......conditions will make life miserable". Similar are the speculations about the moon and the earth and their ages. The false and wrong assumptions and the baseless postulations on the part of the men of sciences in the above quotation are quite obvious. The sun, or the universe is a wonderous creation of the Supreme Lord, created for a definite divine purpose, and it will disintegrate or fade away in the manner chosen by the Lord Himself after the fullfilment of the divine goals. Sura-i-Qiamat. the Resurrection of the holy Quran predicts the disintegration of the entire cosmos after the occurence of a specific cosmic phenomena of the eclipse of the moon. A new small chapter has, therefore, been added to this book captioned as "The Cosmic Hazards of the planet earth". This chapter deals with the predictions of the Holy Quran about the eclipse of the moon, heralding the doom of the earth itself.

All the prophets and the messengers of Allah who have come from time to time to this world, have reminded the humanity that there exist in the highest unreachable interstellar spaces promised lands and gardens for the abode of righteous people of the planet earth and that the law of just returns operates in this world and in the hereafter and that there are invisible universes besides the present one in which we live, and that the life of the human soal does not end here on this planet but it continues, on the contrary, to sour higher and higher to a destined goal. The Holy Quran enjoins upon us to repattern our life to the revealed straight path set forth for the entire human race, and to strive for the attainment of a blissful life here and the hereafter. In the words of the Holy Quran.

> Does man think
>
> That be will he left
>
> Uncontrolled (to do all sorts of mischief)
>
> Was he not a drop
>
> Of sperm emitted (in lowly from)?
>
> Then did he became
>
> A leech-like Clot;
>
> Then did (God) made, and fashioned (him)

In due proportion
And of him He made
Two sexes, male and female
Has not He (the same)
The power to give life to the dead?

Sura-i-Qiamat.

Sd. Abdul Karim Chippa,
Karachi.

Dated. 1st November 1971.

بِسْمِ اللهِ الرَّحْمَنِ الرَّحِيْمِ

CONCEPTION OF GOD

In the name of Allah, the Beneficient, the Merciful

Say: O Allah! Owner of Sovereignty! Thou givest sovereignty unto whom Thou, wilt, and Thou withdrawest sovereignty from whom Thou wilt, Thou exaltest whom Thou wilt and Thou abasest whom Thou wilt. In Thy hand is the good, Lo! Thou art Able to do all things.

Thou causest the night to pass into the day, and Thou causest the day to pass into the night. And Thou bringest forth the living from the dead, and Thou bringest forth the dead from the living. And Thou givest sustenance to whom Thou choosest, without stint.

Quran (Sura-i-Al-Imran)

We pray for the Mercy of Allah upon the prophet of Islam and his followers. May Allah shower His Mercy upon Mohammad the greatest teacher and leader of humanity for all times to come-Amin !

During the dark ages prior to the Holy Prophet's birth, the whole world had sunk into barbarism because mankind had distorted completely the notion and true concept about God; instead of worshipping one God, they had begun to adore and deify numerous false gods, consequently paganism, atheism, and pantheism, all opposed to single Godhead, had their sway. According to A. Yusuf Ali:

"For the glory of Hellas, and her freedom and wisdom had departed;

Rome's great systems of law, organisation, and universal citizenship had sunk into the mire of ecclesiastical formalism, and dogmatism, and exclusive arrogance;

The living fire of Persia's Prophet scarce smouldered in her votaries of luxury;

In India, countless castes and kingdom cancelled the unity of Buddha's teaching;

> The wounds of China had not yet been healed by Tang culture;
> And Japan was still a disciple of China."

The Holy Prophet (peace be on him), when he began to preach his doctrine of the Unity of God, was face to face with severe challenges and with multi pronged attacks of the paganistic world. Allah, out of His infinite mercy revealed the famous Sura-i-Akhlas (Pure faith) which emphatically declared the unity of God, and refuted all the false doctrines.

> Say: He is God
> The One and Only
> God, the Eternal Absolute (all depend upon Him
>   and He depends upon none)
> He begetheth not, nor is He begotten
> And there is none
> Like unto Him.

All philosophy, all metaphysics, and all sciences that man has known since the past ages have shown and proved ultimately the eternal truth and verities, embodied in this Sura. The Holy Quran itself, to a certain extent, is a commentary on the above verses, the truthfulness of which has been vindicated and upheld throughout the historic ages. The Holy Prophet (peace be on him) had disseminated the true doctrines in a surprisingly short time and cut short the polemic and philosophical discourses on the single Godhead; he had declared the fact that God and His nature cannot be defined, and that to have a true concept about the nature of God, man should ponder over the attributes of Allah and create within himself such good qualities and traits attributable to Him. Doctor Khalifa Abdul Hakim writes in his book 'The Islamic Ideology,' page: (83:) "If the conception of God is narrow or false then the attitude for submission, far from leading to well being, would make life narrow and perverted. Every worshiper assumes the complexion of the object of his worship. The God, we are asked to submit to is Wise, Rational and Good and His traits are Love and Mercy. The submission to such a God implies, in attitude and in action, regulations of our own lives. God, according to Islam, is not a Dogma but an Ideal and a regulative of Life. God is the guarantee of our highest values. The same writer says (page 86:) "Religion then, according to Islam, is nothing more than that a man should actively and effectively believe in God as the Creator, and a Rational and Moral Order in the Universe and in the human life and as the origin and promulgator of Laws, which are the laws of the Preservation of values, and the maintenance and richment of well being. It is his duty to discover this God within himself and within the Universe in general"

The Holy Quran contains beautiful pieces which reveal more than hundred Divine names. God manifested Himself in the Holy Quran through His names, and invocation and contemplation over these Divine names on the part of the faith-

fuls, creates a sort of divine presence in the heart. The Universe
is the other thing manifesting some of the aspects of the Divine Being. We humans cannot comprehend and know all
the traits and attributes of Allah and His Divine Essence
(Zatt). Let us, therefore, look for the traits of allah in the
passage known as Ayatul Kursi, Surah Al-Baqar in order to
have a true concept of God.

> *..God! There is no God but He:
> The Living, as the Self Subsisting Eternal:
> No slumber can seize Him nor sleep
> His are all the things in Heaven:
> And on earth
> Who is there who can intercede in His presence
>   except as He permitteh:
> He knoweth what (appeareth) to
> His creatures as before or after
> Or behind them (He knows all the secrets)
> Nor shall they compass Aught of His:
> Knowledge except as He Willeth:
> His throne doth extend over the heaven and the earth;
> And He feeleth no fatigue:
> In guiding and preserving them:
> For He is the Most High,
> The Supreme (In Glory),"

The above Quranic verses convey the meanings that all
the things that are in the heaven or in the earth or in between
them, belong to the only Supreme Sovereign and that man
can have limited right to use or right of possession under the
doctrine of the Sovereignty of God over all the things.

---

*Holy Quran, by A. Yusuf Ali.

4

Allah is the Preserver of all the values. Any attempt at aggression or destruction of the values of life is a crime against God and humanity. Man is the vicegerent of God holding in trust the things of life. The second obvious meanings is that one who believes in the life of the hereafter, will see for himself that his salvation does not lie in the promise, often made by priestly order, to intercede and intervene for him before the Almighty for the condonment of his sins, cruelties and tyrannies practised in this mundane life. Every soul is liable for his deeds of omission and commission, resulting from an injudicious exercise of discretionary powers; or powers exercised in direct opposition to the free will, with which every one of us is armed. No body, however, high, he may be, can intercede save when permitted by the Divine Powers themselves. The above verses put the last nail in the coffin of the claims of the so called Divines and Holy men and Pirs to intercede before God. According to the Holy Prophet (peace be on him) pious deeds and prayers are the best recommendations for a person in the life hereafter. The Holy Quran elucidates this point further and brings out the purposeful creative powers of God in Surah Najm. (star).*

> "Nay: Is He not acquainted:
> With what is in the Book
> of Moses. . . . .
> And of Abraham
> Who fulfilled his engagement?
> Namely, that no bearer
> of burden can bear
> The burden of another,

---

*Holy Quran, by A. Yusuf Ali.

That man can have nothing
But what he strives for;
That the fruit of his striving
Will soon come in sight;
There he will be rewarded
With a reward complete;
That Thy Lord
Is the final goal;
That it is He who;
Grants laughters and tears;
That it is He who
Grants Death and life;
That he did create
The pairs—Males and females;
From a seed when lodged
(in its place)
That He hath promised
A second creation
(raising of the dead); That it is He who;
Giveth Wealth and Satisfaction;
That He is the Lord
Of Sirius (The Mighty Star)."

One should not draw the conclusion from the above verses that· God is arbitrary, and capricious, creating the universe without the casualty; and that man is without the free will. Theologically speaking, 'he Divine Being is self-diffusing Good, Beauty, Wisdom, Love. Dr. Ishrat Husein, who expounded the metaphysic of Dr. Iqbal writes in this context (page 77:) "God's infinite power is not revealed in the arbitrary and the capricious but in the recurrent, the regular and the orderly. Divine will essentially moves in the direction of the good". He further writes "the phenomena of pain and visible evil helps us to realise our, egohood (self conciousness) and to persist in our aspirations for perfection. Evil or pain are not to be regarded as absolute. They are relative to our success or failure in our attempt to perfect our egohood and personality." In other words God moves invisibly to reconstruct values of life through a dialectical process. Hence difficulties which we consider as evils accompany our opportunities, discomfort and ease go together.

The last verses refer to Sirius--the object of worship in the paganistic world. Recent discoveries in the field of astrophysic have shown that the Star Sirius is a White Star, its component having the greatest density of matter so heavy that seemingly an square inch of its matter will weigh upto two or three tons in weight; it is in one of the degenerating category of stars in the process of decay. As against this there are giant red star on the other side of our galaxy which are in the process of development. According to astrophysicists, the new stars in the galaxies originate in gas, grow old, and die in accordance with the physical laws. The sun, the moon, and the earth according to this theory of Science, will in future fade away when HEAT DEATH takes place. Sirius, the star in question is in an advanced stage of decay. Thus the false gods of the pagans are to fade away and the falsity of the belief of the unbelievers will stand exposed. The verses under reference are the aphorisms which give lie to the theory held by many that the fate of an individual is predestined. It is this theory which the Holy Quran attacks and assails. It declares that

"Man can have nothing
But what he strives for."

The profound significance of the Quranic thought lies in its practicability and dynamism, unlike the pernicious dogmas held by the cynic or the fatalist who thinks that he will be reduced to nothing after the separation of the body from the soul.

The wild speculations of the men of Sciences are important to note here. They believe that matter is indestructible and as such, man can exist after his death in the form of scattered atoms in the whole of the universe. Professor H. Levy in his booklet "The Universe Of Science", writes, "At a very remote epoch in the past it would seem that a large and swiftly moving star swung suddenly from outer regions of space into the range of attraction of the sun, and in its passage a mass of hot gas was torn from the sun's side. From such an accident, as it is sometimes called, was the Earth born; although, indeed, it is no more an accident than any other event in the universe. Whether accident, design, or sheer necessity, however, the materials that compose your flesh, blood and bones were, at one time, many million miles away from here in the heart of the sun. Every human body is, in fact, a mottled mass of molecular history, and the blueness of its blood or the lowliness of its origin shows itself socially rather than chemically. We are not merely internationalists, we are universalists."

Professor H. Levy views the world of Science in a perpetual state of renewal, and affirms the religious fact "That outside and above science there is said to be an Absolute Purpose in the Universe, and it is the function of human endeavour to uncover it. There is a Supreme Dialectician who knows not merely every infinitesimal detail of the universe, but appreciates it as the interlocking, interpenetrated whole that it is. This absolute Unchanging Being strives to guide us into the path of goodness or drives us from the path of wickedness. The human soul, in so far as it reflects the divine purpose, is supreme over matter; man is free and master of his destiny."

For our purpose the last phrase of Prof. H. Levy has deep significance. Doctor Khalifa Abdul Hakim in his book "The Metaphysics of Rumi", summing up the views of Maulana Roomi on predestination elucidates this point further. (Page 7) "Predestination is true so far as the Laws of God are concerned. Individual choice is not predestined; the form of Law is eternal: its content is free and variable————. The laws of nature hold good for all times and, therefore, metaphysically expressed, they are out of time and theologically expressed, they are predestined————. (1) Destiny has written once for all that every action shall have reaction corresponding to it. If you choose a crooked path, the inexorable law of Destiny would lead you into error. (2) Injunctions, prohibitions, praise, blame and reward and punishment would be mockery if the doer of action has not been free to choose. (3) Struggling and striving does not mean striking one's head against fate, because it is the very fate of man to struggle. Struggling against the destiny is the very destiny of man."

Certainly man is the architect of his fate and a free agent to shape his destiny but the modern stress and strain of life and environmental factors have chained him and made him a creature of the circumstances. The Holy Quran seeks to remove his chains and unload him from the load of false gods, false desires, false and pernicious doctrines, putting on the modern garb of facism, imperialism, racialism, capitalism

and communism. The Holy Quran is very clear on this point
(page 3880:)*

> 'Those who follow the Apostle;
> The unlettered Prophet:
> Whom they find mentioned
> In their own (Scriptures):—
> In the law of the Gospel:—
> For he commands them
> What is just and forbids them
> What is evil; he allows them
> What is lawful and as good
> (And pure) and prohibits them
> From what is bad (and impure);
> He releases them;
> From their heavy burdens;
> And from the yokes,
> That are upon them
> So it is those who believe in him, honour him
> Help him and follow the Light
> Which was sent down with him.
> It is they who will prosper.''

A passing reference must be made to the Holy Prophet
Mohammad (peace be on him), who alone established a truely
working democratic social order in the beginning of the 7th
Century A.D., in him materialised the dreams of Plato who
visualised a philosopher king, putting the disorganised and
confused affairs of mankind into an ideal order and setting,
bringing it into line with a welfare state. The Holy Apostle
and his revered associates were the true vicegerents of God

---

*Holy Quran, by A Yusuf Ali.

10

on earth. History records about their simplicity and natural ways as under:—

"When Abu Bakr succeeded to the leadership, and the world in its entirety came to him in abasement, he did not lift up his head on that account, or make any pretensions; he wore a single garment, which he used to pin together, so that he was known as the 'man of the two pins'. Umar Bin Al-Khattab, who also ruled the world in its entirety, lived on bread and olive-oil; his clothes were patched in a dozen places, some of the patches being of leather; and yet there were opened unto him the treasures of Chosroes and Caesar. As for 'Uthmen, he was like one of his slaves in dress and appearance; of him it is related that he was seen coming out of one of his gardens with a faggot of firewood on his shoulders, and when questioned on the matter he said, 'I wanted to see whether my soul would refuse'. When 'Ali succeeded to the rule, he bought a waistband for four dirhams and a shirt for five dirhams; finding the sleeve of his garment too long, he went to a cobbler and taking his knife cut off the sleeve level with the tips of his fingers; yet this same man divided (or distributed) the world right and left. Al-Kharras, Sufism by Prof: A. J. Arberry, (page: 32.)

In the Holy Quran, there occurs the Arabic Word "Ummi"—which has been translated as unlettered. The Holy Prophet (peace be on him) was unlettered but possessed at the same time the highest wisdom. It must be added, however, that the claim of the Holy Quran to divinity and miraculousness rests primarily on the experience of direct perception; and secondly upon the fact that the Apostle of God being unlettered, received direct revelations,—the celestial light, without the intermediaries of written words or signs *i.e.* without any earthly creature as an agent. Thirdly, upon the natural rhythm, music and cadence, linguistic beauty, and flow in the Holy Quran which is unsurpassable and matchless; hence the inimitability of the Quranic Verses.

Fourthly, the natural and true faith relied entirely upon divine revelation which is free from the biased, tainted, and doubtful knowledge possessed by the then contemporary world of the Holy Prophet (peace be on him).

Fifthly, upon the prophecies of the Holy Quran that have turned out to be true and fulfilled, or are in the process of being fulfilled. The Holy Quran makes it abundantly clear that divine and supernatural powers intervene in the historical events to establish justice or fair-play. Besides, there are several factors which we cannot discuss here in this booklet, upon which rest to a certain extent, the miraculousness of the Holy Quran.

To Dr. Iqbal, it must be mentioned, the Holy Apostle was like this:

> "The Prophet, power and strength of soul and heart,
> Becometh more beloved than God himself;
> His book is reinforcement to the heart
> Of all believers through his wisdom flows
> The life blood of the whole community
> To yield his garments hem is death."

Let us resume the subject of attributes of Allah after this slight digression. To define God and his divine nature is an imposibility for there exists none conceivably, who could be compared or likened unto Him. According to the Holy Quran the things and their nature visible and invisible, created by God are so large and varied that nobody can reduce them

12

into writing, even if all the trees and their branches spread over the world, are employed as pen and water of a whole sea, supplemented by seven seas, as ink.

Sura-i-Hashr ends with a very beautiful passage, bringing forth some of the chief attributes of God. The passage refers to a mountain which would have humbled and reduced itself to dust for fear of God, had it possessed self consciousness like humans and pondered over the deep meanings of the Holy Quran. Allama Yusuf Ali renders this passage into English as under:—

"Had We sent down

This Quran on a mountain,
verily, thou would have seen
it humble itself and cleave.

Asunder for fear of God.
Such are the similitudes
Which We propound to men,
That they may reflect.

God is He, than Whom
There is no other god;
Who knows (all things)
Both secret and open;
He, Most Gracious,
Most merciful.

God is He, than Whom
There is no other god;
The Sovereign, the Holy One,

> The source of Peace
>   (and Perfection),
> The Guardian of Faith,
> The Preserver of Safety,
> The Exalted in Might,
> The Irresistible, The Supreme.

Mohammed Pikhtall, a new convert to Islam and a European, renders the same passage into English (page 732).*

"He is Allah than Whom there is no god. The Knower of the Invisible and the visible. He is the Benficient the Merciful. He is Allah, than whom there is no god. The Sovereign Lord, the Holy One, Peace, the Keeper of Faith, the Guardian, the Majestic, the Compeller, the Superb. Glorified be Allah from all that they ascribed as partner (unto him). He is Allah, the Creator, the Shaper out of naught, the Fashioner. His are the most beautiful names. All that is in the heavens and the earth glorifieth Him, and He is the Mighty, the Wise.

Yet, Prof. A.J. Arberry a Christian orientalist has poured, his labour over the Holy Quran* and translated this exquisite passage:

> "He is God;

> There is no god but He.

> He is the knower of the Unseen and the visible;

---

*The Glorious Quran.

‡The Koran interpreted by Prof. A.J. Arberry.

14

He is the All-merciful, the All-compassionate.

He is God:
There is no god but He.
He is the King, the All-Holy, the All-peaceable,
The All-faithful, the All-preserver
The All-mighty,the All-compeller,
The All-sublime.
Glory be to God, above that they associate !
He is God,
The Creator, the Maker, the Shaper,
To Him belong the Names Most Beautiful.
All that is in the heavens and the earth magnifies Him;
He is the All-mighty, the All-wise.

Hence, it is clear that the Holy Quran is untranslateable
and inimitable, the actual Arabic text is so supurb that a repeated recital or reading of the passage under refernce, creates
a divine presence in the heart and ecstasy and a hypnotic effect.
Aldous Huxley, in his Book "The Door of Preception", has
prescribed masculine drug to create a sort of ecstasy in order
to transport the self into the antipodes of the mind, as a measure to escape from the stress and strain of the modern hard
life.   Had he known the Arabic text of the Holy Quran, read
and understood, he would have made a rare discovery that the
divine and the supernatural book, the Holy Quran possesses
all the remedies for the spiritual illness of the soul.

Sura-e-Hadid commences as follows :—(Page 1497;)*

Whatever is in

____

*Holy Quran, by Allama Yusuf Ali

The heavens and on earth,—
Let it declare
The Praises and Glory of God :
For He is the Exalted
In Might, the Wise
To Him belongs the dominion
Of the heavens and the earth :
It is He Who gives
Life and Death; and He
Has Power over all things.

He is the First
And the Last
And the Immanent;
And He has full knowledge
Of all things.

The above are some of the verses of the Holy Quran from which some attributes of God can be known but the Quranic picture of the attributes of God, who is Unpicturable and inconceivable is incomplete without quoting Dr. Khalifa Abdul Hakim. In his book "The Metaphysics of Rumi" (page 128), he writes on the authority of the Holy Quran "(1) He is the Creator Who creates things out of nothing, by a sheer act of will. When He desires to create a thing He only says, 'Let it be,' and there it is.   He is an Artist (but not in the sense of the Greek thinkers):   He creates Matter as well as Form. He created the Universe and the angels, before He created man.

(2) He is the incessant source of life; everything and every body or being exists and persists through Him.

(3) He is endowed with the highest attributes.

(4) God is the only self-subsisting, eternal and necessary Being and everything else is created and has a contigent existence.

(5) He is immanent as well as transcendent. Inspite of the fact that everything lives through Him, nothing is like him and He transcends everything; He cannot be contained by the Universe and cannot be bound by time and space. He is Immanent, because He is in everything and specially in the soul of man, because it was His own spirit which He breathed into man.

(6) Every thing except His own Being is perishable.

(7) The whole Universe is His revelation, but He reveals Himself more directly and personally to His chosen creatures to guide them and the others through them.

(8) He does not incarnate Himself ; no man, be he the most perfect among men, can ever rise to be equal to God The infinity of God's knowledge and power are immensely superior to anything attainable by man

(9) He sees and hears and speaks and replies and can come into the closest personal touch with His chosen ones. He tries men and rewards virtue and punishes vice. He acts with justice and with truth, but His will is inscurtable though he acts according to definite unalterable ways.

(10) God is the Light of the heavens and the earth, His

knowledge comprehends every thing in the heavens and the earth. Nothing is hidden from Him and the slightest movement does not escape His notice.

(11) The physical eye cannot see Him."

The picture of the Universe, emerging after scientific investigation, is a picture which is incomprehensible, incapable of being measured and, therefore, defies description. According to John Langdon Davies who writes in his 'book, 'The Man and His Universe, that if a man travels with the speed of light, i. e., 1,86,000 miles per second, supposedly for a period of 14 crores of years to see the whole Universe, he cannot do so; since the whole of the universe is so vast and majestic, that many of the expanding parts thereof are not as yet exposed to human view. Those parts, which are exposed to our view through electronic devices are so large and colossal interconnected, and organic whole that a sense of nothingness of the earth deepens in our heart. So the picture of the universe that science has drawn has turned out to be inconceivably greater and incapable of being visualised. Hence, how Magnificient and Majestic is the Loving Wise God, the Creator, the Sustainer, the Cherisher, the Protector How unpicturable and even intellectually incomprehensible is the Providence?

The Holy Quran describes the absolute power and control of the Divine Being over the universe in symbols and anthromorphically as under :—Sura-i-Zumr, page : 1256.*

No just estimate

---

*Holly Quran, by A. Yusuf Ali

Have they made of God,
Such as is due to Him :
On the Day of Judgement
The whole of the earth
Will be but His handful,
And the heavens will be
Rolled up in His right hand :
Glory to Him !
High is He above
The Partners they attribute
To Him !

The Trumpet will (just)
Be sounded, when all
That are in the heavens
And on earth will swoon,
Except such as it will
Please God (to exempt)
Then will a second one
Be sounded, when; behold,
They will be standing
And looking on !

And the Earth will shine
With the glory of its Lord,
The Record of (Deeds)
Will be placed (open) ;
The Prophets and the witnesses
Will be brought forward ;
And a just decision
Pronounced between them ;
And they will not
Be wronged (in the least).

Elsewhere, in the Holy Quran, we come across the chief attributes of God who is Omnipotent, All-powerful and All-knowing. To God, the function of creating and recreating the whole of the Universe is very easy like the creating and raising again of a single soul. We end this chapter with the praise of Allah by S. A. Hussein.

O Thou ! the Life and soul of all we see,
Thou who wilt last when all else will die,
Thou who broughtest into being this world,
Roofed with the blue expanse of Heaven fair.
Adorned with countless, golden Lustrous eyes,
And lamps, all night that burn illuminating
This universe, Thou who art Life and Light

PRAYERS AND THEIR USEFULNESS

The Holy Quran is a synthesis of all the divine books and its fidelity to the scriptural truths and fundamentals is very extraordinary. The present atomic and space age is characterised by the unhappy and lamentable lack of pure faith and true belief in one God, one humanity and one world—the true ideology for which the Holy Quran stands. Man of to-day generally speaking, is suffering from the chronic imbalance between his material and spiritual values ; emphasis is more on material things of life at the cost of his spiritual well-being, thus his spiritual link with his Creator has been weakened for want of proper prayers on his part. The lack of true religiousity, arising out of his unhealthy materialistic pattern of life, has made him an atheist in the modern society which is itself divorced, to a great extent, from morality and true religion.

The question arises, why one should hold true faith, pray in the orthodox manner, and do good deeds? The answer to this impertinent question can be sought in the Holy Quran which asserts, firstly, that man being the crown of creation, possessed of necessary will power, and higher consciousness, has been the recipient of utmost fovours of his Lord, Who has enabled him to have control over himself and over the external phenomena, or over nature.

Surah-i-Luqman, declares

"Do ye not see
That God has subjected
To your (use) all things
In the heaven and on earth,
And has made His bounties
Flow to you in exceeding (measure),
(Both) seen and unseen
Yet there are among men
Those who dispute about God.

Elsewhere, in the Holy Quran, we learn that invocation of Divine names creates a kind of divine presence in the heart "therefore, Remember Me, I will remember thee," Be thankful to Me and don't reject Me"; "Surely, the Salat (Prayers) prevents a man from undesirable actions and evil deeds and the invocation (rememberance) of Allah and His divine names (Zikr) is a great thing ; Or, "Be constant in your prayers during the times at both ends of the day and during a part of the night ; surely, good deeds drive out the evil ones. This Holy Quran is for those who invoke His names constantly or remember Him"

Secondly, man has entered into a binding contract with his Creator prior to his physical appearance on this earth to the effect that God is the only All-powerful Lord (Rabb), Providence, Sustainer, the Cherisher, the Preserver, exclusively worthy of our object of worship and adoration; having no patron, partner, equal associate, or any comparable. Objection may be raised that man is quite ignorant of any preternatural life, and so he cannot remember the contract, if any, that might have taken place prior to his physical appearance in this world or before his birth.

Molvi Mohd. Ismail, Shaheed (Martyr) has written a very thought-provoking journal on the subject of Shirk—that is, to ascribe partners, equal, and patron to God. This journal has been translated into English, entitled 'Support of the faith'. The Quranic version of the covenant or contract is described by this journal as follows :-

"And when thy Lord drew forth their posterity from the loins of the sons of Adam, and took them to witness against themselves, saying 'Am I not your Lord? they answered, 'Yea, we do bear witness'. This was done lest ye should, at the day of Resurrection, say, 'Verily, we were negligent as to this matter, because we were not apprised thereof'; or lest ye should say, 'verily, our fathers were formerly guilty of idolatry, and we are their posterity who have succeeded them: wilt Thou therefore, destory us for that which vain men have committed"—Surah "Aaraf"

According to Molvi Mohd. Ismail, shirk or to ascribe partners to God, or panthiesm is the highest and the most heinous crime, or unpardonable guilt in the sight of God. As the Holy Quran, declares that false gods other than the true God, possess no power :

*"O Men! Here is
A parable set forth!
Listen to it! Those
On whom, besides God,
Ye call, cannot create
(Even) a fly, if they all
Meet together for the purpose !

---

*Holy Quran by A. Yusuf Ali.

And if the fly should snatch
Away anything from them,
They would have no power
To release it from the fly.
Feeble are those who petition
And those whom they petition !

The clear meanings of the above verses are that a section of men who enjoy all the joys of life and material comforts go out to worship idols, or graves of saints, pirs, and ascribe their success to the secret help of such false gods or persons other than true God. They, in fact, flagrantly abuse their reason, intellect—they therefore, commit the unpardonable guilt, mentioned in all the true scriptures, (page 870:)*

'Yet they worship, besides God,
Things for which no authority
Has been sent down to them,
And of which they have
Really no knowledge :
For those that do wrong
There is no helper.

According to the Holy Quran, man was created to adore and worship his Creator, who alone sustains and cherishes all things and the same are entirely dependent upon His grace, mercy and justice. If the human beings rebel against God by being ungrateful, they are doing so against their own interest or against their own nature. Man, therefore is naturally bound to bow to the natural laws, as such he is under a binding contract with his Creator to worship Him. To prove this we

____

Holy Quran, by A. Yusuf Ali

take the analogy of a son and his mother. The son cannot deny the fact of his birth from his mother, whom he is bound to help and respect, although he possesses secondary evidence regarding the fact of his birth from a particular female *i.e.* his mother. A Christian cannot deny his baptism solemnised by his parents while he was still an infant. So in the like manner, a man cannot wriggle out of the binding contract which took place between him and his Creator prior to his appearance in the physical form in this world—on the plea of ignorance. Secondly, we have to acknowledge the truthfulness of this scriptural fact on the testimony of a galaxy of eminent prophets, apostles, saints, and men of piety, who have come and gone reminding humanity of this contract and the responsibility of the humans for their acts of omission and commission before their Creator on the day of judgement. Surely, man is answerable before his Lord for all his evil doings.

Thirdly, man adores and worships his Creator because his natural urge and his inner self so dictate him. While praying he conveys his sense of gratefulness for all the love and beneficience of God of which he is the recipient. The Holy Quran lays great emphasis on the institution of Salat (a system of congregational prayers five times a day) and Zakat, (a system of Charity). The institution of Salat (Congregational prayers) is very conducive in the fostering of a sort of spiritual socialism; and the institution of Zakat, and the Quranic law of inheritance, are the most useful constituents or factors in the removal of social inequities in the economic spheres; it prevents the concentration of wealth in the hands of a few. While the institution of Hajj, which enjoins upon the faithful to perform pilgrimage once in a life time, to the Holy places of Macca and Madina, is chiefly meant to foster a spirit of universalism and enhances and facilitates the establishment of an ideal international brotherhood of men on this earth. Lastly, the institution of fasting for a full month in each year is meant to inculcate the habit of forbearance, tolerance and patience in the face of hunger. In short, all the Islamic institutions are meant to improve the social order in all the fields. Mr. Mazheruddin Siddiqui, in his book "MARXISM OR ISLAM" writes "Islam Recognises the Law of Nature, that a community cannot remain healthy and vigorous in which the mass of people are proverty-stricken and in which there are great inequalities of wealth and fortune. Therefore, Islam prescribes Zakat (poor-tax) and abolishes interest. In the social sphere the law of nature is that a community cannot maintain its bodily health and intellectual vigour if it falls a victim to sexual immorality Therefore, Islam forbids adultery, prescribes marriage and permits polygamy, if certain conditions are fulfilled. For the same reason it prohibits drinking, because the habit of drinking ultimately involves those addicted to it in sexual immorality. In the international sphere the experience of mankind teaches us that a world divided by racial, tribal and national loyalties can prosper neither materially nor spiritually. Therefore Islam recognises no distinction of race, nationality and tribe and builds its social fabric on a universal basis which cuts across national and racial loyalties. In the external sphere we find that a community which adopts a contemplative attitude towards life in contrast with the active, and develops too great inwardness of thought.neglecting the outer world and the practical necessities of life, succumbs sooner or later to more active communities. Therefore, Islam forbids monasticism and prescribes Jehad which covers the conquest of nature, control of external forces and a struggle against the evils of social environment. In the sphere of inner life, it is an inevitable social law that if a community becomes too much engrossed with the other world and devotes itself exclusively to the control of external forces forgetting the necessity of self-control and the need of self-conquest, it soon creates social conflicts within itself. Therefore, Islam enjoins prayer and fasting, teaches fear of God and inculcates belief in the after-life for the purpose of moral self control." The Holy prophet, therefore, (peace be on him), laid great stress on the observation of congregational prayers five times a day. According to him the Salat (prayers) is the outstanding feature of a true believer; it distinguishes a believer from a non-believer, and it is a sure remedy for his spiritual ills: Salat, therefore, confers peace of mind and tranquility of heart upon the devotee. The physical movements of the body like bowing, kneeling and prostrating in reverence are the practical expressions of a slave's utmost sense of humbleness and his feelings of gratefulness towards his Creator.

According to the messenger of Allah, Salat (prayers) transports a devout servant into the highest spiritual realm—Meraj.

Fourthly, all the Holy scriptures of great religions speak about a life in the hereafter, where man's destiny will be fully realised, and the divine purpose for which man has been created, will materialise. Faith, and prayers, supported by good deeds are the corner stones on which stands the whole spiritual edifice in this world and the life beyond.

Fifthly, man has several natural urges and instincts; according to Dr. M. Rafiuddin, the low instinct of sex or hunger is dominated by the higher drives or urges for beauty, knowledge, love, and ideal.   There is yet another predominant and basic drive in man, to know his Creator and love Him.   The latter urge, to know the Creator, becomes more pronounced in the advancing years of a man's life.   To know the Divine Being is to love Him; to love is to pray and prostrate and submit ones will to the Universal Will.   According to the Holy Quran man has to strive hard in this mundane life in order to prepare himself to meet his Creator in the life of the hereafter to account for his good or bad deeds.   Man, therefore, has to believe in the law of just return for his deeds and actions.   Those persons who are spiritually alive, have a definite goal of seeking the Divine Being and strive hard to attain their goal through right prayers, adorations, and rituals.   Right prayers prescribed by the Holy Quran and Holy Prophet (peace be on him) are the essentials of a true and dynamic faith, mere professions of which lead one to no-where; certainly, a prayer bears fruits if it is performed with an intent that conforms to its meanings, The Holy Prophet has said "The value of action is only through its intentions". Writing on the efficacy of prayers Tetus Buckhardts, in his book "An Introduction To 'The Sufi Doctrine', now translated by Matheson, says, (page 124) "The Divine names revealed by God Himself imply a Divine presence which becomes operative to the extent that the names take possession of the mind of him, who invokes it.   Man cannot concentrate directly on the Infinite but the concentrating on the symbol of the Infinite, attain the Infinite itself."

Dr. M. Rafi-uddin, writing on the subject of prayers in his book 'Ideology of the Future' (page 87 :) says.

"Unfortunately, we have not yet understood the real significance of our desire for prayer. It is the most powerful and the most important urge of human life making its first push for an outlet along the only channel that can offer it a free, full and continued expression. It is the desire of beauty pressing for satisfaction. It is the crossroad sign of nature leading to the road of happiness. It is the voice of nature calling man to freedom, progress and power, If we listen to this voice, it becomes louder more eloquent and more explicit and talks out to us the secrets of existence, the meaning of human life and the purpose of the Universe. If we stifle this voice, we give ourselves up to error and ultimate distress and sorrow which must persist so long as we do not listen to it again. We cannot escape from ourselves; it is impossible for us to shed our own nature".

To stress this point further, we also quote Professor James, who writes:

"It seems that inspite of all that Science may say or do to the contrary, men will continue to pray to the end of time, unless their mental nature changes in a manner which nothing we know should lead us to expect. The impulse to pray is a necessary consequence of the fact that whilst the inner most of the empirical selves of a man is a self of the social sort yet it can find its adequate socius (its great companion) in an ideal world. Most men either continuously or occasionally carry a reference to it in their breasts. The humblest outcast, on this earth can feel himself to be real and valid by means of this higher recognition. And on the other hand, for most of us, a world with no such inner refuge, when the outer social self failed and dropped from us, would be the abyss of horror. I say for most of us because it is probable that men differ a good deal in the degree in which they are haunted by this sense of an ideal spectator. It is a much more essential part of the consciousness of some men than of others. Those who have the most of it are possibly the most religious men. But I am sure that even those who say that they are altogether without it deceive themselves and really have it in some degree".

According to the Holy Quran, all the things visible and invisible, organic and inorganic that are in the heavens or in the earth, glorify God, Who holds every one by its forelock. Those who don't pray and prostrate, their shadows do the protrasting; all the created things seen or unseen follow natural laws and cooperate in the fulfiling of the Divine purpose. The unbelievers who don't have faith in God and in his promise of a life in the hereafter have no legs to stand, and in the words of the Holy Quran :

> "Seest thou not that
> To God bow down in worship
> All things that are
> In the heavens and on earth,
> The sun, the moon, the stars;
> The hills, the trees, the animals;
> And a great number among
> Mankind?   But a great number
> Are (also) such as are
> Fit for punishment : and such
> As God shall disgrace,
> None can raise to honour :
> For God carries out
> All that He wills".

30

According to Dr. M. Rafi-Uddin, a life without prayers and adoration is an unnatural and abnormal life, led in direct conflict with the inner self, or the basic urge in man. This abnormal life brings with it the evil consequences of bodily and mental diseases like Neuroses and the diseases of the heart. The Holy Quran as a whole is full of commandments to maintain institutions of Salat (a system of constant congregational prayers five times a day) and the institution of zakat (a system of charity), and to enforce the Quranic Law of inheritance. These institutions were or are in fact the main pillars of the edifice of the whole Muslim civilizations. The Holy Quran declares in clear words that the fall of ancient civilizations was brought about by ignoring the commandments regarding the institutions of prayers and charity; these civilizations and their people ignored the fundamentals and the essentials of the true religion and quarrelled over forms, rites, rituals and over formalities. The test of a true religion is that its institutions and doctrines possess universalism and endeavour to unify the whole world into an unbreakable system of universal brotherhood of men, removing the distinctions of race, colour or country, subordinating regional loyalties to the higher demands of the society and the good of the world. The Holy Quran emphatically announces the oneness of the whole human race in Surah-i-Hujrat (page 1407) :*

> "O Mankind ! We created
> You from a single (pair)
> Of a male and a female,
> And made you into
> Nations and tribes, that

____

*Holy Quran. by A. Yusuf Ali.

Ye may know each other
(Not that ye may despise
Each other).   Verily
The most honoured of you
In the sight of God
Is (he who is) the most
Righteous of you.
And God has full knowledge
And is well acquainted
(with all things).

The same sura declares the universal brotherhood of man
and makes practical suggestions to maintain the brotherhood
of men and of nations, and chalks out a practical method by
which international disputes can be solved through peacful ne-
gotiations and arbitrations or through applying military sanc-
tions against the transgressing nations by the united nations
or International Organizaticns, when all the means fail.

If two parties among
The Believers fall into
A quarrel, make ye peace
Between them : but if
One of them transgresses
Beyond bounds against the other,
Then fight ye (all) against
The one that transgresses
Until it complies with
The command of God;
But if it complies, then
Make peace between them
With justice, and be fair :

> For God loves those
> Who are fair (and just).
> *Surah-i-Hujrat (page 1405)*

It must be mentioned, that the entombed mighty old civilizations, now being excavated in several parts of the world, speak eloquently about their past glory and about their evil fate of total extinction : these were ruined because of the materialistic pattern of life, and these were devoid of true faith, prayers, and good deeds.

The past Muslim regimes dating back to the good old days of Khilafat-i-Rashida, were characterised by intense faith and religious fervour,and strict adherence to tenets and commandments of the Holy Quran; consequently all the Muslim nations who followed the Quranic Ideology rose materially and spiritually to unprecedented heights of glory; but unfortunately these nations entered into the dark ages due to ignoring the Quranic teachings in letter and spirit.   The huge and majestic old mosques and buildings, still standing and scattered in Asia and Europe, tell tales of old glory, and of righteousness of the devout Muslims, submitting to the will of God.

Today man's power to undo himself knows no bound and his baseness knows no limit, but for the fear of nemises and God's vengeance through the operation of the law of just returns, he is within certain limits. There comes a time in every civilization when a system af Quranic checks and balances become imperative and God's invisible hand, very subtle and rarified, corrects the decaying society and restores the original spiritual well being and other higher values of life through the

*Holy Quran b A. Yusuf Ali

slow dialectical process of construction, destruction and reconstruction. The Holy Quran declares "If the Huq (Almighty) allows man's (aggresive) desires to materialise, (the forces of earth come into clash with the forces of heavens). Consequently, all that lies between them comes to naught". Sura-i-Al-Mominoon. Hence, we sadly note that at this stage of the history of mankind, nations and individuals are restless and in a perpetual state of mobility, and afraid of each other; and the big powers are putting up threats of a nuclear war to devastate the whole globe. These signs are nothing but the evil consequences of an exclusively materialistic Godless civilization of the Western or Eastern Hemisphere. These point out the abnormality and artificiality in the modern civilization, lacking true religiousity and spiritual sensivity. The remedy lies in restoring the lost values of religion and morality and in reviving the old institutions of prayers and good deeds and in restoring the pure faith in one God, one Humanity and one world, and in a belief in the life of the hereafter.

MEANINGS OF SURAH-I-FATEHA (Opening chapter)!

—:o:—

Let us now turn to the Quranic prayers known as (Surah-Fateha), the first chapter of the Holy Book. This chapter constitutes the essence of the Holy Quran, and 'the quintessence of Islam', It is often repeated on all congregational prayers and on solemn occasions. According to the Holy Prophet (peace be on him) no Muslim prayers (Salat) whether congregational or otherwise, is complete if Surah-i-Fateha is left out from recitation. This short and sweet chapter sets forth the true conception of an universal religion and fundamentals of the scriptures. The whole book of the Holy Quran is a commentary on this most important chapter, consisting of seven small verses.

It must be mentioned here that Mr. Gandhi used to recite this Sura-i-Fateha in public prayers. We know on the authority of Mira Ben that Mr. Gandhi even copied the Holy Prophet (peace be on him) in the matter of food, which consisted of milk and dates for some time, and prayers during the last watches or hours of the night; but it is sad to think that his followers have completely forgotten and set aside the lessons of non-violence taught by this great Hindu leader of the Indian subcontinent, and who was greatly influenced by the universalism and dynamism of the Quranic thought.

The chief characteristic of this opening chapter is that it contains no personal note of individualism but is permeated with a spirit of universalism; it depicts the human nature which is prone to be misguided and misled by false gods and false desires; in short it is the most appropriate address from the humans to the Creator, the all Merciful God, asking for His mercy and grace;

Surah-i-Fateha (Opening Chapter)

In the name of God, the Merciful, the
Compassionate

Praise be to God, the Sustainer of the worlds,

The Merciful, the Compassionate

Lord of the Day of Judgement

Thee (alone) do we worship and Thee (alone)

Do we ask for help

Guide us on the straight path,

The path of those on whom Thou has bestowed
Thy Grace

Not (of) those upon whom is (Thy) wrath and who
Have gone astray

Allama Yusuf Ali, renders this most important chapter into English as follows:

In the name of God, Most
Gracious. Most Merciful
Praise be to God
The Cherisher and Sustainer of the worlds;
Most Gracious, Most Merciful;
Master of the Day of Judgment.
Thee do we worship
And Thine aid we seek.
Show us the straight way
The way of those on whom
Thou hast bestowed Thy Grace
Those whose (portion)
Is not wrath,
And who go not astray.

It must be stated here that Maulana Azad* has written a book entitled Ummul Kitab in which he has commented at length on this chapter of Surah-i-Fatiha; this commentary has been summarised by Ashfaque Husain, Bar-at-Law, in his book namely "The Quintessence of Islam", in which he has brought forth the fundamentals of true religion, deducible from this chapter in question and has reduced the same in the following lines which we take the liberty to quote at length:

____

*We do not agree with him (Maulana Azad) in political matters, because he clearly worked against Muslims interest in pre-partition days, and was the greatest opponent of the true Muslim ideology which our revered Quaid-i-Azam pursued until his death.

(a) "To have a correct conception of the attributes of God. The errors into which man has fallen in his worship of God have all emanated from his misunderstanding of God's attributes.

(b) "To believe in the law of just returns. Everything in the world has particular properties and a natural effect, and so men's actions also have certain properties and effects; good actions lead to good and evil actions to evil.

(c) To believe in life after death. Man's life does not end in this world; life will continue beyond it and man will continue to reap the returns of this actions.

(d) To recognise the path of rectitude and grace".

Mr. Ashfaque Husain further sets forth on the authority of Late Maulana Azad in the clearest possible terms the basic spiritual lessons from the opening chapter of the Haly Quran:

(1) One of the greatest spiritual errors of man has been to conceive of God as an awesome and terryfying being rather than as love. The sura, therefore, begins with Hamd, adoration through praise, there is no reference to any fearsome aspect of divinity.

(2) The first attribute of God referred to is that of Rabbil-Alammeen, the Cherisher, Nourisher and Sustainer of the universe, and it contains two lessons, it tells man of God Who gives him all he needs by way of sustennace, material and spiritual, so that he may protect himself from all evil and proceed to his full development, secondly, it tells him that God is the

God of the Universe, not of any part of it.   There is
no room left for any narrow-mindedness prejudice
and exploitation, whether individual, tribal, commu-
nal, racial, national, religious or of any other kind.
His grace and gifts are for all mankind, not for any
particular group or any particular religion.

(3)   He is the Lord of the Day of Judgement. Firstly, He
is the Supreme Judge; to none else it is given to sit
in judgement upon man. Secondly, there is a Day of
Judgement or reckoning. Man must be prepared to
face the consequences of his acts, as he expects every
thing else to have a known, natural and inevitable
effect. Thirdly, man should expect only justice, the
due result of his acts; God is neither arbitrary nor
revengeful.

(4)   In making submission to Him and acknowledging
and seeking His help it is not said merely that we
worship him and seek His help. It is said instead;
"Thee (alone) we worship; and Thee (alone) we ask
for help." Not only has it fixed the relationship between man and his Lord but it has also proclaimed in
unequivocal terms tne unity of God, and it closes all
paths to polythism, in whatever form.

(5)   The path of profit and grace is described as the
straight Path. The Straight Path is easier to
recognise and follow, and the more one deviates from
it the greater the danger of one's going astray.

(6)   Often, however, it is not easy to distinguish which is
the straight path. Man is helpless, for the answer to

the question is hidden in the womb of the future and he can but proceed on the basis of his very limited knowledge and very restricted reason. He can then but seek the grace of God and pray; O Lord, direct us on the right path; "the path" for I know not which it is "of those on whom Thou hast bestowed Thy grace, not of whom who have brought upon themselves Thy wrath and have gone astray."

Hence, the Surah-i-Fateha constitutes the core, heart, and the essential of the Muslim Prayers. We must note here that God out of His infinite Mercy has revealed the Holy Quran, which points out the right path, we ask for.

We also take the liberty to quote hereunder the Quranic prayers, the most beautiful and sublime, for our readers without any comment.

(Pray:) "Our Lord!
Condemn us not
If we forget or fall
Into error; our Lord!
Lay not on us a burden
Like that which Thou
Didst lay on those before us;
Our Lord! lay not on us
A burden greater than we
Have strength to bear.
Blot out our sins,
And grant us forgiveness,
Have mercy on us.
Thou art our Protector:

Help us against those
Who stand against Faith
Sura-i-Al Baqara :

—:o:—

"Our Lord! not for naught
Has Thou created (all) these!
Glory to Thee! Give us
Salvation from the penalty
Of the fire.
Our Lord! Any who Thou
Do'st admit to the fire
Truely Thou coverest with shame,
And never will wrong doers
Find any helper.

Our Lord! we have heard
The call of our calling
(Us) to faith, to believe
In the Lord, and we have believed.
Our Lord!
Forgive us our sins
Blot out from us,
Our inequities,
And take to Thyself our souls
In the company of the righteous.

SCIENCE AND THE HOLY QURAN !

(a) Origin of the Universe :

There are numerous verses in the Holy Quran which throw some light on the theory about the origin of the universe, which is under scientific investigation. The Holy Quran, it must be admitted, was revealed to the Haly Prophet (peace be on him)some thirteen hundred years back during a period of twenty three years, It embodies religious and scientific truth on the one hand, and philosophical and metaphysical truth on the other hand; it contains numerous references to the sciences of sociology, cosmogony, physics, cosmology and human psychology. The Holy Quran exhorts the humans to study nature and its mute fundamental laws. Having, enunciated the fundamental theory of the unity of God, it prepares the ground for the discovery of the uniformity of natural laws, operating in the universe. According to the latest scientific views, matter is indestructible: when the matter is in motion it assumes several forms, like heat, light, electricity, energy, vapour, gas, and smoke. According to the theory of relativity propunded by the famous Scientist Dr. Albert Einstein, Energy $=$ MC2 *i.e.* energy is equal to Mas in motion of velocity of the light 183,000 p.s.). There are numerous verses in the Holy Quran which lend support to the scientific theory that the universe was in a gasuous state prior to its condensation to the present shape of the earth, a satellite of the solar system. The Holy Quran is explicit on this point.

"And it (universe) had been (as) smoke :
He said to it and to the earth".
"Come ye together,
Willingly and unwillingly"
They said we come
(Together) in willing obedience
So He completed them
As seven firmaments
In two days *i.e. two periods and He
Assigned to each heaven
Its duty and command
And we adorned
The lower heaven
With lights (and provided it)
With guard, such
Is the decree of Him
The exalted in Might
Full of Knowledge. Surah-i-Sajdah (Prostration).

Hafiz Ghulam Sarwar renders the same passage into English as fallows :—

"Then he (directed His vital Force (will) towards the (Universe) and it was a gas (smoke)!"

He then said to it and the earth (come ye both, willingly and unwillingly. They replied We both come willingly).

Then he converted it into seven heavens (heavenly bodies) each having day and night and to each of those seven heavens

____

*According to the Holy Quran 'one day' is equal to one thousand years. or 50,000 years of our earthly existance, for pre-eternal life cannot be measured by days months or years of earthly life.

42

(heavenly bodies) He assigned a special task, We (God) decorated the space of this earth with lamps and safeguard.

This is the determination of the Al-Mighty, Al-knowing.

The gist of the Quranic verses is that the whole universe is one, and was created by one God. According to Carlyle the whole universe cooperates in producing a single blade of grass. The organic wholeness of the universe is amply demonstrated by the following verses :—

Have not those who disbelieve in God, consider that heavens and the earth were one mass joined togther) then We (God) cleaved them as under : And we made every living thing form Water. Will they not even believe now? The verses under reference give support to the scientific truth that all life whatever its, form, originated in water when the earth, a part of the sun itself cooled down to the level of water.

The evolution of man

———

We believe that every Quranic verse dealing with the evolution of human species, or animal life, cannot be fully understood without reference to the sciences of biology and physics which have developed phenomenally in the present age. The famous orientalist Dr. Nicholson has rendered into English the theory of evolution, propounded by the saintly Moulana Rumi, who Illustrated the descent of the soul into matter and its ascension to its divine origin on the authority of the Holy Quran.

"The moment thou to this low world wast given,
A ladder stood whereby thou mightest aspire;
And first thy steps, which upwards still have striven,
From mineral mounted to the plant; then higher

To animal existence; next, the Man,
With knowledge, reason, faith, O wonderous goal !
This body, which a crumb of dust began—
How fairly fashioned the consumnate whole !

Yet stay not here they journey: thou shalt grow
And angel bright and home far off in heaven,
Plod on, plunge last in the great Sea, that so
Thy little drop make oceans seven times seven.

'Thy Son of God!' Nay, leave that word unsaid,
Say, 'God is One, the pure the single Truth'!
What though thy frame be withered, old, and dead,
If the soul keep her fresh immortal youth?

The Holy Quran describes the evolution of Man as
under :—

Men we did create
Form a quintessence (of clay) ;

Then We placed him
As (a drop of) sperm
In a place of rest,
Firmly fixed ;

Then We made the Sperm
Into a clot of congealed blood ;
Then of the clot We made
A (foetus) lump ; then We

44

Made out of that lump
Bones and clothed the bones
With flesh; then We developed
Out of it another creature.
So blessed be God,
The Best to create!
After that, at length,
Ye will die.*

The Holy Quron's emphasis on the study of sciences.

———

The Holy Quran lays great emphasis on the study of nature and its phenomenas, which are subject to uniform laws, operating in them. A close study of these natural laws is always rewarded with the discovery of profound scientific truths.   The Holy Quran says ; (page 173 :)

Behold! In the creation
Of the heavens and the earth,
And the alteration
Of night and Day,
There are indeed Signs
For men of understanding,

Men who celebrate
The praises of God,
Standing, sitting,
And lying down on their sides,

*The Darwinian theory of the evolution of man and animal is correct to a certain extent. But it is a blasphemy to consider that no Divine purpose governs our existence and that the Vital Force has no say in the survival selection, and evolution of man or animal.

> And contemplate
> The (wonders of) creation
> In the heavens and the ear th.
> (with the thought) :
> "Our Lord! Not for naught
> Hast Thou created (all) this !
> Glory to Thee! Give us
> Salvation from the Penalty
> Of the fire......Surai-i-Al-Imran.*

The Holy prophet (peace be on him) had exhorted all his followers and particularly the learned and the intellectuals to contemplate over the mysteries of nature, and in God's wonderfull handi-work. According to holy traditions an hour's contemplation over God's beautiful creation is equal to a whole year's prayers: Any good act done honestly is equally a n act of worship of Allah: An honest workcr who is a beleiver in one God is also a friend of Allah'.   Dr. Iqbal in his book "The   Reconstruction of Religious Thought in Islam", writes.

"The scientific observer of Nature is a kind of mystic seeker in the act of prayer. Although at present he follows only the footprints of the musk-deer, and thus modestly limits the method of his quest, his thirst for knowledge is eventually sure to lead him to the point where the scent of the musk gland is a better guide than the footprints of the deer.* This alone   will add to his power over Nature and give him that vision of the total-infinite which philosophy seeks but cannot find. Vision without power does bring moral elevation but cannot give a lasting culture. Power

---

*Holy Quran, by A. Yusuf Ali.

46

without vision tends to become destructive and inhuman. Both must combine for the spiritual expansion of humanity."

What Dr. Iqbal means to convey is that power without vision, that is, material prosperity and material comforts without spiritual well being, will lead the humans to a dead wall. The western materialistic Godless pattern of life has led the world to two disastrous holocausts and may God forbid, when the threat of a nuclear world war materialises, it will wipe out human race from this earth. The Holy Quran contains numerous verses whose import is to exhort thinking section of humanity to study the seen in order to know the Unseen, which is a stark reality. Surah Yaseen is clear on this point : Page 1117.*

> "A sign for them
> Is the earth that is dead :
> We do give it life,
> And produce grain therefrom.
> Of which ye do eat.
>
> And we Produce therein
> Orchards with date-palms
> And vines, and We cause
> Springs to gush forth therein :
>
> That they enjoy
> The fruits of this (artistry) :
> It was not their hands
> That made this :
> Will they not then give thanks ?
>
> Glory to God, Who created

———————————

Holy Quran, by A Yusuf Ali

In pairs all things that
The earth produces, as well as
Their own (human) kind
And (other) things of which
They have no knowledge.

And a Sign for them
Is the Night: We withdraw
Therefrom the Day, and behold
They are plunged in darkness ;

And the Sun
Runs his course
For a period determined

For him : that is
The decree of (Him),
The Exalted in Might,
The All-Knowing

And the moon,
We have measured for her
Mansions (to traverse)
Till she returns
Like the old (and withered)
Lower part of a date-stalk.

It is not permitted
To the sun to catch up
The moon, nor can
The Night outstrip the Day :
Each (just) swims along

In (its own) orbit
(According to Law.

And a Sign for them
Is that We bore
Their race (through the Flood)
In the loaded Ark ;

And we have created
For them similar (Vessels)
On which they ride

If it be Our Will.
We could drown them,
Then would there be
No helper (to hear
Their (Cry), nor could
They be delivered,

Men being, the crown of creation, the vice-gerent on
this earth is armed with the weapon of a free will, or what
we call, the self conciousness, began to lead a civilized life
on this earth some ten thousand years back. He being thinking and goal seeking human, in whom Allah had breathed
"HIS SPIRIT", had been asking himself from the very
beginning "What am I here for? why I live and suffer in
this world"? In other words he began to investigate the
very divine purpose for which he was created. The Holy
Quran which contains within itself the teachings, and
wisdom of all the prophets and their wise utterances,
answers the above questions of man adequately, and
convincingly.

We are living in this age of scepticism, craze for power

and pelf, and in an age of technology, science, and space. There are hundred and one mysteries of nature which the probing mind of the modern scientist or the philosopher has failed to unravel. We do not know whether this earth is egg-shaped or pear-shaped ; how this earth, the satellite of the solar-system, separated itself from its nuclei. Whether the stars we see are dead stars or live stars: Whether there are signs of life in them or not Whether the universe is expanding or contracting*? These, and many are the questions that are engaging the attention of cosmogonists and scientists.

It must be mentioned here that the ascension of the Holy Prophet (peace be on him) into the limitless space, mentioned in Surah-i-Asra (The Night Journey) was a unique phenomena in the astronomical world. The significance of this historical event lies in the fact that man is capable to conquer the space and even go beyond, and is certain to couquer the same in due course of time to come. The Holy Quran in its first chapter, known as Surah-i-Fateha refers to Rabb (Providence, or Sustainer), to Whom belongs all the glory and grace as the Lord of the worlds. Not only this but in several chapters of the Holy Book, we come across verses like the following :

"So Glory be to God. the Lord of the Heaven and of the earth, and of the worlds". God knows better, but from all these we conclude that there exist numerous other worlds, which are not exposed as yet to human eyes. Sciences of cosmogony and cosmology which have made rapid strides in the sphere of knowledge, shall one day discover other worlds.* — — — — — — — — — —

---

*According to the Holy Quran the Universe is expanding (see Surah-i-Zarriat) We (God) made this cosmos with power and we are expanding it.

* Sura-i-Rehman speaks about worlds in heavens full of beautiful lands and gardens, and bounties of Allah, meant for righteous people

-referred to in the Holy Quran, which lays great emphasis on the study of sciences.

Significance of Sura Ar-Rehman

The Holy Book throws a practical challenge to man's technical knowledge and to his intellectual and spiritual powers in Surah Rehman one of the most poetic chapters of Holy Quran. This Surah begins by referring to the Divine Name of Rehman, the Gracious, who created man, taught him the Holy Quran, granted him the power of expression or speech. It also refers to the harmony and the order prevailing in the universe, in which the sun, moon, stars, and the trees follow natural law, and bow themselves before the divine purpose. The Surah under reference also speaks about the natural resources and means of sustenance and reservoirs of food and poses a pertinent question repeatedly thirty one times. "Then which of the favours of your Lord will ye and ye deny" It must be added that certain commentators think that the Holy Prophet's ascension into the heavens was made divinely feasible because therein lay a further proof of the confirmation of the divine revelation, which the Holy Prophet received from time to time.

The chapter in question *i.e.* Surah-Rehman draws the attention of man towards the divine order and harmony in the natural phenomena. Since there prevails complete balance and a wisely visioned order in the act or motion or movements of the heavenly bodies, so in the same manner man, the wonder-creation, and his social order should move and act in harmony with the divine purpose, removing all the imbalances that have crept into his spiritual and material values. In the present world we find there is a chronic disorder in the form of abject poverty and backwardness in the

East on the one hand, and opulence and excessive material comforts in the West at the expense of spiritual values, on the other hand. In other words the conquering of the space and ascendancy in the cosmic field by the big powers, largely depend upon the removal of this chronic imbalance in our spiritual and material values. The challenge, we presume, to the technology and scientific knowledge of man and to his spiritual powers is in the following words of the Holy Quran. and God knows better :—

> "O ye assembly of Jinns
> And man if it be (feasible)
> Ye can pass beyond
> The zones of heavens
> And the earth, pass ye
> Not without authority (power or knowledge.)
> Shall ye be able to pass
> Then which of the favours
> Of your Lord will ye and ye deny ?

This challenge was thrown some thirteen hundred years back after the ascension of the Holy Prophet (peace be on him): But with the advent of Islam there has been a continuous growth in the scientific knowledge of men, who, to their credit, have harnessed most of the natural forces for their daily use, and in times to come their probe into the cosmos will bear fruit in the discovery of new worlds. According to the Holy Quran, the sun, the moon, the stars, and the space and the wind and all the natural forces are servants, and subservient to humans, who, in the words of the Holy Quran. quarrel with theiv Lord, and draw for Him parallels from the created things. Surah-i-Yseen is clear on this point (page 1187.)*

52

"Do not man see

That it is We Who

Created Him from sperm ?

Yet behold ! He (stands forth)

As an open adversary !

And he makes comparisons

For Us, and forgets his own
(Origin and) Creation :

He Says, "Who can give

Life to (dry) bones

And decomposed ones (at that) ?

Say, He Will give them

Life Who created them

For the first time?

For He is well versed

In every kind of creation !"

We are subject to correction as some commentators of the Holy Quran differ from the interpretation which we have put upon the verses relating to the space or zones of the heavens and the earth.

Science has discovered for us radio waves which carry our voice to the four corners of the earth seven times in a second ; even our beat of the heart to any destination : They even carry our photos and televise our actions. According to latest discoveries, we are surrounded on all sides by invisible currents and waves of ions, electrons, magnetism, radio waves

---

*Holly Quran, by A. Yusuf Ali

and a host of other cosmic rays that are found in the strata-sphere, above the earth. According to the Holy Quran, the man, the miracle of nature is being watched, protected, and guided by secret agents, who, we presume, record and televise the action of man on the divine glass fixed in the higher realm, invisible to the physical eyes of the mortals. The heavens above, and the earth, under our feet is criss-crossed by hidden waves in tne manner of a net work of electric and telephone wires in a modern city.*Surah Zarriat (page 1421:*)

"By the heavens, which is of the nature of a net work ' or by the sky with its numerous paths.

Truðly you are in a
Doctrine Discordant

The purpose of the Quranic verses dealing with the probe of nature, or investigation into scientific truth is to energise and enliven the dead heart, and to uncover the realities of life and its potentialities; to fire mans' imagination, intellect, intuitve powers and create in him a true and vigorous spirit of inquiry and investigation into the seen and the unseen; to enlighten man's path leading to truth and Ultimate Reality.

Surah-i-Luqman declares
"Do ye not see
That God has subjected
To your (use) all things
In the heavens and on earth

*See 'The Philosophy of the Holy Quran' by Hafiz Ghulam Sarwar.
*Holy Quran, by A. Yusuf Ali.

54

And has made His bounties
Flow to you in exceeding
Measure (both)
Seen and Unseen
Yet there are among men
Those who dispute about God
Without knowledge, and without
Guidance, and without a Book
To enlighten them

The Holy Quran contains numerous references to general sciences and lays emphasis on vision, intellect, rationality. The Arabic Language of the Holy Quran is the language of the reason and a spiritual language of the heart, read, written and understood in all the four corners of the earth. The specific divine word or 'speech' is distinct from the conventional Arabic prose or poetry or language. It creates a special symphony, rhythm, and lyrical inwardness' in the soul of man possessed of true faith in Allah and in His promise. It creates in the heart of man the requisite spiritual ecstasy and stillness to enable it to soar into the unknown regions, or antipodes of mind, and into ecstasic states of mind, which cannot be described by any word, term, measure and symbol.

The so called orientalists*, with a few exceptions, are not possessed of pure faith in God and in His Holy scriptures, who pose to interpret the Holy Quran and Hadith of the Holy Prophet (peace be on him); they in fact cannot do their job faithfully since they lack intellectual honesty

---

*They neither believe in the Unity of Apostlehood, nor in the finality of the Holy Prophet of Islam (peace be upon him)

required of them The divine message embodied in the Holy Quran has reached to non Muslims through-out the globe through foreign agencies and men who were biased and who followed the materialistic pattern of life, divorced from true religion and real ideology for which the Holy Quran stands.

MYSTERIES OF LIFE !

Let us revert to the problem of the origin of life and its mysteries. Science has shown since the 19th century that cells are the most important structural units of living tissues. It has been learnt that most cells consist of protoplasm and a nuclei, surrounded by a cell wall and that the nucleus contains its own protoplasm chromatin and genes. Science has established that genes are the master molecules, which regulate how fast or slowly a cell reproduces, whether it shall be a cell suitable for a plant, or fish or animal, whether it will be a cell used in the stomach, the liver, the muscles, blood or parts of the body and the characteristics it inherits from its ancestors. Dr. T. D. Casperson, the noted Swedish Scientist has proved that all cells whether human, animal, plant, have one primary function in common. The synthesis of the amino acid which makes up protein. Every kind of cell whether of a tree, animal or man has to produce the protein on which tissues, muscle, and organs feed. He has also discovered that wherever a cell reproduces by dividing into two, the concentration of nucleic acid increases. This increase, he has shown, is particularly noticeable in the rapidly growing tissues of the human embryo. He has also demonstrated that the nucleic acid (there are many) have a strong bearing on the hereditary properties of the genes Dr. Casperson was able to record photographically cellular details through his intricate instruments developed by himself and known as Micro-Spectro Photo Metre. But it must be noted that all the cell and the cellular minute details, the handiwork of God, have defied the highly developed micro-spectre; and hence much of the cells makeup and their activities is a total mystery to science. For instance the following questions still remain unanswered- (See 'the life of Dr. Casperson' in one hundred most important people).

"What is the chemical substance in the genes that detemines whether a child's hair will be red or or black ?

Why do the cell multiply more rapidly as the child grows and less rapidly at maturity ?

Why do the cells sometimes start to grow in an uncontrolled manner and end up as a fatal cancer.

What is there in the cell that gives it life ?
We may add a further question. Why and how the mode of thinking and the mode of writing, and even the manner of weeping or laughing takes hereditary characteristics ? According to the Holy Quran the mysteries of life shall remain unsolved because man was granted limited divine knowledge, Surah Asra, declares :

"They ask thee concerning
The spirit (of inspiration).
Say" The spirit (cometh)
By command of my Lord
Of knowledge it is only
A little that is communicated
To you (O Man)

We have thus seen that the cellular activities and their working is controlled by the unseen forces : The cells and the atoms whose nature and mode of behaviour, controlled by the natural laws, we presume constitute the hidden armies and the invisible forces of God operating in and dominating over the human minds. The Holy Quran declares in Surah Muddassir (page 1644) :*

> Thus doth God leaves to stray
>
> Whom He pleaseth, and guide
>
> Whom He pleaseth : and none
>
> Can know the *forces*
>
> *Of the Lord*
>
> Except He
>
> And this is (Quran) no other than
>
> A warning to mankind

SIGNIFICANCE OF SURAH-I-YUSUF !

Science has proved beyond doubt that even the tiniest atom moves and acts in an order, for example the electron moves in an orbit round its nuclei. The 'forces of God consisting of atom and electrons which give birth to molecules and cells the basic material for life, are subservient to the natural law. The brain cell are the chief cells controlling other cells, operating in the lower part of the body, like the muscles, the liver, the kidney etc. They move in unison to give vitality and vigour to the organic life. These atoms and their electrons have a lesson for humans who form into family units, communities, nations and a single international

---

*Holy Quran, by A. Yusuf Ali.

58

social order. The father and the mother, or elders in the family are the nuclei of the human atoms and the sons, the daughters and the youngsters are the electrons, revolving round their nuclei, the sun (the parents). But the irony of the present day circumstances is that the modern society is taking its base on the disintegrated family unit all over the world, providing ample material to aesthetic writers for writing human tragedies, atrocities, tyrannies so characteristic of the present-age. The Holy Quran advocates for and puts emphasis on the joint and integrated organised family unit, which was the backbone of healthy societies in the good old days, providing a kind of social insurance against unemployment, destitution, and disabilities of certain family members.

In Surah-i-Yousuf (Joseph) (peace be on him), we come across the prophetic dream of Joseph, the description of which is very beautiful, for the Holy Quran likens a good family to a solar system (Sun moon and stars), father, mother, sons and daughters.   (Page 550):*

> "Behold, Joseph said
> To His father
> "O my father
> I did see eleven stars (in dream)
> And the Sun and the moon
> I saw prostrate themselves
> To me".

This dream of Joseph (peace be on him) came true when his eleven brothers and the partiach Jacob (peace be on him)

---

*Holy Quran, by A. Yousuf Ali.

and his wife prostrated themselves before him after a score of years when the family reunion took place. Joseph (peace be on him) had attained a high position as a Governor in Egypt, was previously deserted by his half brothers. In any society in order that it may attain stability, its members must *move* and act in harmony and in union in the manner of solar system or like the electrons and the atoms round their nuclei. This harmonious movement of the solar system is further described in Surah Yasin :

    And a Sign for them

    Is the Night : We withdraw

    Therefrom the Day, and behold

    They are plunged in darkness ;

    And the sun

    Runs his course

    For a period determined

    For him : that is
    The decree of (Him)

    The exalted in Might

    The All-Knowing

    And the Moon
    We have measured for her

    Mansion (to traverse)

    Till she returns

    Like the old)and withered)

    Lower part of a date-stalk

    It is not permitted

To the sun to catch up
The moon, nor can

The Night outstrip the Day
Each (just) swims along
In (its own) orbit
(According to Law)

He, Joseph (peace be on him) fell a victim to the jealousy of his half brothers, But Yousuf (peace be on him) foresaw his bright future and showed unprecedented broad-minded liberality, and tolerance in cementing again the family tie, once torn asunder by his half brothers on account of their cruelties and tyrannies against their own brother. The significance of Surah-i-Yousuf lies in the fact that our own Holy Prophet (peace be on him) foresaw his most brilliant future. One who possesses sterling character, and qualities of heart and head, and a honesty of purpose, can carve out his own destiny.

THE BEAUTY OF THE HOLY QURAN

It must, however, be mentioned that the Holy Quran embodies a dynamic and forceful message for a true world ideology, which can unify and knit together the whole divided world into a single international society. This divine message is contained not only in books, but stands engraved upon the hearts of thousands of Huffaz (those who remember by heart the whole of the Holy Book in its Arabic text.) The witchery of the "Divine Speech" of the Holy Quran and its Arabic wording is such that tears course down the cheeks of faithfuls in a state of ecstasy and rapture when they attempt recitation repeatedly of the Holy Book. Professor A. J. Arberry praises the Holy Book in the following words : "Briefly, the rhetoric and rhythm at the Arabic of the Quran, are so characteristic, so powerful, so highly emotional that my version, whatsoever, is bound in the nature of thing to be, but a poor copy of the glittering splendour of the original. Ibn Rushd has said that the divinity and miraculousness of the Arabic Text of the Holy Book rests upon the direct evidence of perception. For this reason the Holy Book is a living miracle of this world to this day. The Holy Quran poses pertinent questions to mankind as a whole, in Surah Abasa.

> Woe to man !
> What hath made him
> Reject God ?

From what stuff
Hath He created him ?

From a sperm-drop :
He hath created him, and then
Mouldeth him in due proportions :

Then doth He make
His path smooth for him,

Then He causeth him to die,
And putteth him in his Grave :

Then, when it is
His will, He will
Raise him up (again)

By no means hath he
Fulfilled what God
Hath commanded him

Then let man look
At his Food
(And how We provide it) :

For that We pour forth
Water in abundance,

And we split the earth
In fragments,

And produce there-in Corn

And Grapes and nutritious plants,

And olives and Dates,
And enclosed Gardens,
Dense with lofty trees.
And Fruits and Fodder,

For use and convenience
To you and your cattle

Then again in Surah Infitar (the cleaving as-under):—

O Man ! what has
Seduced thee from
Thy Lord Most Beneficient ?—

Him Who created thee,
Fashioned thee in due proportion,
And give thee a just bias ;

In whatever Form He wills,
Does He put thee together.

Nay! but ye do
Reject Right and Judgement !

But verily over you
(Are appointed angels)
To protect you,—

Kind and honourable,—
Writing down (your deeds)

> They know (and understand)
> All that ye do.

Surely, the Holy Quran is right. The harnessing of electricity, the radio, and micro-waves for the purpose of conveying the sound to the four corners of the earth by man, is a distinct feat of achievement which add feathers to man's hat. So in like manner, we presume, our actions are televised and recorded by a secret agent namely the suh-concious mind as a proof positive for use in future, in case, we are abusing the free will, the intellect, with which we are endowed.

Science has proved that the universe is so vast and majestic that if a man travels in space by the speed of light for crores of years, he cannot even then see the whole of the universe. There are millions of stars bigger than the earth itself, which float in space in a complete order, and disciplined manner. There are thousands of galaxies or clusters of galaxies, occupying limitless space but all these move in a systematic measure in accordance with the divine scheme of things. The powerful electronic devices have failed to periscope the vast universe, of which the earth itself is a minute part like a white dot on a leaf of a crotone tree, and its white dots on its leaves, illustrate in a partial manner the cosmos and the heavenly bodies in the interstellar space above; the universe is like a big tree of galaxy in the cosmos, planted by the divine powers. (the recent achieve ment by the three Americans astronauts, who orbited the moon on the 25th Dec. 1968, Conclusively prove that our earth itself is a tiny star in the vast space.)

The Holy Quran stands for universal brotherhood of men and equality of all nations transcending all the barriers of castes and creed, colour, race and Geography. But the human specei is face to face with a practical threat of extinction through a sudden blast of nuclear weapons possessed by four or five big nations. At the present time ideological war on conflicting, wrong, perverse, and false doctrines, is going on in the world, shattering the old values of morality and religion. As such the comity of nations have to move on harmoniously as a single family of nations like the solar system; the bigger nations are like suns and moons and the lesser as stars, all moving independently in their own spheres in order to survive the ordeal of a nuclear blast. Man has to attain a distinct destiny through the conquering of the space and to unravel the mysteries of the universe. The latest feat of Soveit Russia and the U.S.A., in orbiting men into space is a distinct historical achievement in the conquering of space, and if the probe into limitless space goes on unabated, the day is not distant when man will be in a position to acheive a position of 'elect' through the discovery of new worlds, hinted by the holy Quran But if the scientific achievement in the field of material prosperity is not matched with spiritual and moral attainment, the ascendancy of civilization in the material field will collapse like a house of sand, having no firm ground, in the manner of old civilizations, entombed in all the corners of the earth.

The Holy Quran declares "And He has made subservient to you the sun, and the moon, pursuing their courses, and He has made subservient to you the night and day" (14:32:33).

"And he has given of all you ask Him: if you count Allah's favours You will not be able to number them ; most surely man is very unjust and very ungratefull" (14:34).

It is note-worthy that the idea of space, the vastness of

the space and the idea to split the moon light into two halves, is traceable from the traditions of the Holy Prophet (peace be on him). He had demonstrated that even the sun and the moon are mere agents and servants of mankind, the crown of all creations, the king pin of the universe. The Holy Prophet (peace be on him) had given the notion about the vastness of the cosmos after his space trip (ascension). He told his pious companions that if a horse having the fastest conceiveable speed, that is, if the horse gallops forward very speedily, his single gallop measuring the whole horizon, which the eye can see, and goes on galloping for five hundred years, he can probably reach the first outer space firmaments in heaven, and that there are seven firmaments co-extensive and co-equal. What the Holy Prophet (peace be on him) meant to convey was that the universe is so vast and magnificient that even the human vision and his powers of perception fail to comprehend it. New Scientific investigations have completely changed our picture of the universe, which must be admitted ; and consequently, our attitude towards religion, morality, and conception of God has undergone or is undergoing a radical change, rightly or wrongly.

The Quranic doctrines have stood the test of times, since these are based upon rationality; intellect aud prophetic perception. As regard the beauty of the Holy Quran, Ibne Rushd (Averroes), the metaphysicist and the supporter of Aristotalian Philosophy views the Holy Quran as a living miracle "the most outstanding instance of miraculous deed is Koran, whose miraculousness does not merely rest upon authority, as in the case of converting the stick into a snake, but rather on the evidence of direct perception, and reflection alike. Its unique miraculousness is therefore, so glaringly perceptible, that it can be verified by all men at all times" Kashf (page 73.) (see Muslim occasionalism by Majid Fakhree). The Holy Quran therefore, has a divine and supernatural origin, its authority certified by men of learning, possessing sea-green incorruptibility. As such we find this unique word of God (divine speech), engraved on the heart and mind of millions of men.

We quote in this context Professor A. Guillamine, in his book (Islam), about the Holy Quran, he writes "The Kuran is one of the World's classics, which cannot be translated without grave loss. It has rhythm of peculiar beauty and a cadence that charms the ear. Many Christian Arabs speak of its style with warm admiration, and most Arabists acknowledge its excellence when it is read aloud or recited, it has a most hypnotic effect that makes the listener indifferent to its sometimes strange syntax——————————It is this quality it possesses of silencing criticisms by the sweet music of its language that has given birth to the dogma of its inimitability, Indeed, it may be affirmed that within the literature of Arabs, wide and fecund as it is both in poetry and in elevated prose, there is nothing to compare with it".

As regards rhythm Professor, A.J. Arberry, writes rhythm runs insistently through the entire Koran : but it is changeable fluctuating rhythm ranging from the gentle, lulling music of the narrative and legislative passages through the lively counter-part of the hymns of praise, to the shattering drum rolls of the apoplytplic movements"——————————. Thus to appreciate in appropriate terms the beauty of the language, and the wisdom of the Holy Quran, is but an impossibility.

68

SIGNIFICANCE OF SURAH-I-NOOR!

Let us now refer to Surah Noor (Light).   This is a very exquisite chapter of the Holy Quran the meaning of which is as clear as day light. Its recital indeed, diverts the winged thoughts of men from the impure notions and the false desires in the manner of evening moths who are attracted to the luminous lamps.

"God is the Light
Of the heavens and the earth
The parable of His Light
Is as if there were a Niche
And within it a Lamp :
The lamp enclosed in Glass.
The Glass as it were
A brilliant star :
Lit from a blessed Tree,
An Olive, Neither of the East
Nor of the West,
Whose olive oil is well-neigh
Luminous
Though fire scarce touched it :
Light upon Light !
God doth guide
Whom He will
To His Light :
God doth set forth Parables*
For men : and God
Doth know all things.

The above piece reveals the beauty and the wisdom of the Holy Quran.

---

* The Surah under reference predicts the discovery of electrical lamps and light.

Imam Ghazali (1058-1111) has interpreted these verses to convey the meaning that man's knowledge and power of perception is dependent upon sensory organs, intellect, intuition, and prophetic perception available to him in the divine guidance of the Holy Quran and Hadith of the Holy Prophet (peace be on him). The Apostle of God symbolised in himself the divine-light which dispels darkness of ignorance. Unless man's power for perception is cleansed by following the precept of the Holy Prophet (peace be on him) and by obeying the natural code of morality embodied in the Quran, and the divine guidance, forming the celestial light, referred to in the above verses, he cannot achieve that degree of nearness to the Divine Being or the position of 'elect' for which he is destined. If man develops the inner conviction and retains the true faith, once established by reason, and revelation, avoiding all the pitfalls of futitle metaphysical speculation, with which the present day world is plagued, he can then be in a position to unravel the mysteries, and also unravel the Ultimate Reality. The precept of the Holy prophet (peace be on him), the seal of all Prophets, is the luminous lamp that can lit other lamps or spirits searching for celestial light. The Holy Quran, therefore, puts ideological limits, for there cannot be more than one true world-ideology, namely, one God, one humanity one World, based upon the ideal of universal brotherhood of man, transcending the geographical, racial, and regional loyalties. The Holy Book puts restrictions known as limits of Allah, on the futile speculations, regarding the Divine Being in order to impart order to the chaotic worlds of Ideas and theories by enjoining to keep to the golden middle path, and avoiding the extreme determinism of the Greek Philosophy and the extreme occasionalism of the middle ages, spear-headed by Asharites.

The verses under reference lay down a particular doctrine, which true mystics and saints have tested and found to be true, that a great soul is communicative and diffuses spiritual light among other souls, who are in association, or in close contact with this particular soul *i.e.* the soul of the Prophet. In other words when men of piety and of action, sit together, they impreceptibly inter-communicate sub-consciously with each other in spiritual matters like luminous lamps which can lit other small lamps. The Quranic parable means that if the Holy Quran is read and understood properly, the Quranic light can set aglow a heart, searching after truth independenly of other external circumstances. Mystics and men of learning have testified to this truth of the Holy Quran throughout the historic ages by personal experience , a record of which can be found in the religious literature of the world. Great spirits who are acquainted with each other communicate through dreams and solve the problems connected with difficult situations into which they fall.

This trait of self-communicativeness, therefore, which the pious souls acquire can have corroboration and support from metaphysicits as well. Majid Fakhri asserts in his book "The Islamic Occasionalism" (Page 153), "The Infinity of God's generosity, however, is such that in addition to the perfection of being, He has conferred upon the creature the power to generate being the energy whereby it can communicate its own perfection to other things. And in this is rooted ultimately, the casualty of things, and the dynamic energy whereby they share in the Divine Essence——————
Things tend to be like God for as much as He is God. Now it is out of His infinity that God bestows (goodness) being on others ; for all things act for as much as they are actually perfect." Equally, explicit is sufi Inayat Khan in his Book

(Soofi Message) "And (The prophets) being charged with the ever glowing fire of inspiration from angelic spheres, where they come into touch with angels, they descend to the plane of earth; it is then that their words become tongues of flame, as spoken of in **the scriptures**. This means that every word of theirs becomes a torch, given into the hands of those who listen, to illumine their hearts through light, specially is this so in the life of the great Ones, who have given a divine message, religion, to the world".————————————————The soul of the prophet is a link between the heaven and the earth.

Surah-i-Noor takes a very serious view of the crimes connected with sex and prescribes exemplary deterrent punishment with a view to purify the social order from the poisonous effects which follow as a logical consequence. Those societies which are plagued with sex crimes like, fornication, rape, and adultery, have a very week foundation and are bound to disintegrate sooner or later, despite their material and financial prosperity. This is the reason why the Holy Quran takes a serious view of the sex crimes, for to be guilty of sex crimes is to fall into animism and thereby to destroy the power of perception. According to Holy traditions to commit and to repeat a crime is to blacken the soul and to blur the visionary powers to perceive right from the wrong, and thereby to abuse flagrantly the will power, with which we are endowed. It must be added that the modern night clubs, the films depicting nakedness, obscenity, and scenes of murder, and the pornography executed in the name of art and culture and naturalness, are the powerfull vehicles, employed in the West or in the East on an international plane, to excite sex-crimes and other heinous crimes. To guard and to preserve the moral and ethical values, mentioned in all the new and old scriptures

72

of the world, is the function of every modern welfare state. The Holy Quran points out its finger. specially, towards the sex-crimes which have been the potential cause for the complete extinction of old civilizations. The modern Freudian psycho analytical theory that sex is the basic drive in man is a half truth, a perverse doctrine, and a wrong diagnoses for the spiritual ailment with which the modern society is plagued. It is quite wrong to think that neuroses is the result of resisting this so called basic drive of sex. Neuroses is in fact, the result of leading an unnatural and abnormal life that is, a life divorced from appropriate prayers and true religiousity or it is the result of an unsuccessful life, led in direct clash with the natural urge or ideal for beauty and love, which find satisfaction only in search after truth, or to know the Creator, and love Him through right kind of prayers or worship. (See the Ideology of the future, by Dr. M. Rafi Uddin.)

Surah-i-Noor (light) suggests, some radical remedies for the prevention of sex-crimes, which we cannot discuss here for want of space.

MYSTICISM OF IMAM GHAZALI !

Imam Ghazali, who is the greatest exponent of occasionalism, believes that "prophetic perception is a ken beyond the ken of reason, intellect, or senses "just as it is one of the stages of human development in which there is an 'eye' which sees the various types of intelligible objects, which are beyond the ken of the senses, so prophecy also is the description of a stage in which there is an eye endowed with light such that the unseen and other supra intellectual objects become visible." Imam Ghazali was a mystic, receiving his spiritual powers from the precept of the Holy Prophet and his pious companions. In praise of his mystic experience, he writes (page 60), "Al-Ghazali by Montgomery Watt.") "I learnt with certainty that it is above all mystics who walk on the road of God ; their life is the best life, their method the soundest method, their character the purest character, indeed were the intellect of the intellectuals and the learning of the learned and the scholarship of the scholars, who are versed in the profundities of revealed truth, brought together in the attempt to improve the life and character of the mystics, they would find no way of doing so ; for the mystics all movement and all rest, whether external or internal, bring illumination from the light of the lamp of prophetic revelation; and behind the light of prophetic revelation there is no other light on the face of the earth from which illumination may be received"

There is no doubt that the Holy Quran contains within itself divine guidance for the whole of the humanity, which can illumine hearts provided the latter feed on self luminous olive oil of the Quranic verses and the precept of the Holy Prophet (peace be on him). Imam Ghazali has been much maligned by Western Writers and specially by deterministic theoriticians for his being a mystic and an opponent of casualty. It is quite wrong to consider that he advocated a monkish life. He was convinced of the truthfulness of the Holy Prophet s ʃsayings and the Quranic doctrines. He sought a further corroboration and verification of the doctrinal truth of Islam through mysticism in his old age, and was succesful in his effort to increase his own faith and the faith of other believers; but as the divine power of perception is not possesed by all and sundry but by a few like him; and besides, he could not give expression through adequate words or symbols to his mystic experiences, he has been labelled as the chief sponsor of a negative fatalistic, and meaningless life. Even Dr. Iqbal has not spared him for mysticism. Those who have studied the (Revival of the theological knowledge), Ahyaul-Ulum which is a whole encyclopaedia on theology will find that Imam Ghazali is a quite different figure and a bright luminous star in the intellectual horizon. He has written in the said book that a criminal heart is like a cistern, full of foul water and its sourccs of water are the connected pipes of sensory organs like the eyes, ears, the mind, the mouth and the tongue. The purification of this cistern depends upon the repetitive recitation of the Kalma "La Elaha Illalah", embodying the Quranic doctrine of the unity of God, expressed in the phrase 'There is no god but God and Muhammed is His messenger." According to our Imam a systematic recitation in the prescribed manner will make the cistern (the heart) to give way to a gushing fountain of pure water (spiritual powers) from beneath ; this will throw out the impurities of the cistern and thus a true believer will begin to have a clear perception of all things and the lights celestical will illumine the spiritual self. No saint, or any God-led person, has ever disputed the truthfulness of our Imams' theory, which has been subjected to practical test.

Let us now warn our readers of the dangers, inherent in the perverse theories, held by the modern Pirs and the so called sufies, who indulge in all sorts of follies and orgies of dance and trance, while they claim for themselves union with God or spiritual powers, and who follow a religion of pantheism, which is against the basic concept of Islam. Sufi Inayat Khan whom we have quoted was influenced by the "Incarnation Theory of the Hindus". He propounded the prepostrous novel theory that spirits, when they separate themselves from their bodies soar high into angelic sphere and meet the descending new spirits, who are to be clothed with a body. The former educate and teach the latter lessons for use in their life on earth and for their future behaviour. This is obviously wrong. Had it been the case, the present world would have been otherwise.

It must be mentioned that according to the Holy Quran an average person, who is a believer in one God, need not go deep into theories and practices of the mystics or resort to the monkish life. He is simply to say his conventional congregational prayers while at the same time he should discharge his obligations towards his family, society, nation in order to get the promised salvation in the life of the hereafter.

Mention may also be made of the Book of Prof. A. J. Arbery,* namely Sufism'. He writes that mystics through their mysticism try to attain a state in which they experience a kind of life belonging to the pre-eternal conditions, and that all the mystics concentrate their efforts to reach this

---

*In his book 'Reason and revelation in Islam' he also stated a theory that mystics can have union with God and enjoy ecstastic states of the pre-etrenal life.

state belonging to the pre-eternal life. This is a wrong theory, because the career of a soul consists in moving forward and not in going downward or into digression. Truly speaking, real mystics endeavour to attain a Supra celestial state of blissfulness' which no mortal has ever envisioned. Hence, there are writers who advocate a monkish life. According to the Holy Quran a richer, vigorous, and active life, accompanied by prayers and worship and faith in the Divine Being is the only true life that can be recommended. We, therefore, leave aside this subject of mysticism and quote some beautiful verses of the Holy Quran from Surah-i-Noor in the same context : (page 909). Holy Quran, by Yusuf Ali).

> But the Unbelievers,—
> Their deeds are like a mirage.
> In sandy deserts, which
> The man parched with thirst
> Mistakes for water ; until
> When he comes up to it,
> He finds it to be nothing
> But he finds God
> (Ever) with him, and God
> Will pay him his account ;
> And God is swift
> In taking account.
> Or (the Unbelievers' state)
> Is like the depths of darkness
> In a vast deep ocean,
> Overwhelmed with billow

Topped by billow,
Topped by (dark) clouds :
Depths of darkness, one
Above another : if a man
Stretches out his hand,
He can hardly see it !
For any to whom God
Giveth not light,
There is no light !

According to the Holy scriptures a disbeliever, or a spiritually blind person is like a dead, deaf, and dumb being, because one who is spiritually blind here in this life will remain so in the hereafter. Those who are atheists and devoid of any faith, their good actions even are mere acts of hypocracy having no value whatsoever in the sight of the Lord. According to the Holy traditions, faith and action go together as such faith without action is a dead faith. The above verses show the depth of ignorance of a person without faith, who flagrantly abuses his reason and rejects God in favour of a false god (or false desires) and sells his soul for a mess of pottage. Surah-i-Noor, particularly the verses we have just quoted above, have been subjected to different interpretations by theologians who have sought to give esoteric meanings to these verses but we have not done so. The verses of the Surah-i-Noor or other Surahs reveal the beauty of the language of the Holy Quran.

QUOTATIONS FROM THE HOLY QURAN !

8

The following verses have the deepest meanings like all the other verses, which we quote from the Glorious Quran by Mohd. Pickthall. These verses possess the highest wisdom and the rarest specimen of perceptual beauty, and intellectual integrity, which have deeply influenced the spiritual and social values of mankind throughout the historic ages. These we quote without any comments.

—:o:—

Therefore remember Me, (God), I will remember you Give thanks to Me, and reject not Me.

O ye who believe ! Seek help in steadfastness and prayer, Lo ! Allah is with the steadfast.

And call not those who are slain in the way of Allah "dead". Nay they are living, only ye perceive not.

And surely We (God) shall try you with something of fear and hunger and loss of wealth and lives and crops ; but give glad tidings to the steadfast.

Who say, when a misfortune striketh them : Lo! we are Allah's and lo! unto Him are returning.

Such are they on whom are blessings from their Lord, and mercy. Such are the rightly guided

—:o:—

And of them (also) is he who saith: "Our Lord! Give unto us in the world that which is good and in the Hereafter that which is good, and guard us from the doom of Fire."

—:o:—

O ye who believed! Render not vain your almsgiving by reproach and injury, like him who spendeth his wealth only to be seen of men and believeth not in Allah and the last day. His likeness is as the likeness of a rock whereon is dust of earth; a rainstorm smiteth it leaving it smooth and bare. They have no control of aught of which they have gained. Allah guideth not the disbelieving folk.

The devil promiseth you destitution and enjoineth on you lewdness. But Allah promiseth you forgiveness from Himself with bounty. Allah is All-Embracing, All-Knowing
..................Surah-i-Al-Baqra (Cow)

80

Say : Come, bring your witnessess who can bear witness that Allah forbade (all this).

Say : Come, I will recite unto you that which your Lord hath made a sacred duty for you: that ye ascribe nothing as partner unto Him and that ye do good to parents, and that ye slay not your children because of penury—We provide for you and for them—and the: ye draw not nigh to lewd things whether open or concealed. And that ye slay not the life which Allah hath made sacred, save in the course of justice. This He hath commanded you, in order that ye may discern.

And approach not the wealth of the orphan save with that which is better, till he reach maturity. Give full measure and full weight, in justice. We task not any soul beyond its scope. And if ye give your word, do justice thereunto, even though it be (against) a kinsman; and fulfil the covenant of Allah. This He commandeth you that haply ye may remember.

—:o:—

Say : Lo! my worship and my sacrifice and my living and my dying are for Allah, Lord of the Worlds.

Extracts from Surah-i-Al-Anam

—:o:—

Say (O Muhammad): Call upon those whom ye set up beside Allah! They possess not an atom's weight either in

the heavens or the earth, **nor have they** any share in either.
nor hath He an auxiliary among them.

—:o:—

Whoso desireth power (should know that) all **power** belongeth to Allah. Unto Him good words ascend, and the pious deed doth He exalt ; but those who plot iniquities, theirs will be an awful doom; and the plotting of such (folk) will come to naught.

Allah created you from dust, then from a little fluid, then He made you parts (the male and female). No female beareth or bringeth forth save with His knowledge. And no one groweth old who groweth old, nor is aught lessened of his life. but it is recorded in a Book. Lo! that is easy for Allah.

O mankind! Ye are the poor in your relation to Allah. And Allah! He is the Absolute, the Owner of Praise.

If He will. He can be rid of you and bring (instead of you) some new creation.

That is not a hard thing for Allah.

Surah-I-Fitar (Angels)

—:o:—

For what cause should I not serve Him who hath created me, and unto whom ye will be brought back ?

—:o:—

And when it is said unto them: Spend of that wherewith Allah hath provided you those disbelieve say unto those who believe: Shall we feed those whom Allah, if He willed, would feed? Ye are in naught else than error manifest.

Surah-i-Yaseen

—:o:—

(1) O mankind! Keep your duty to your Lord and fear a Day when the parent will not be able to avail the child in aught, nor the child to avail the parent. Lo! Allah's promise is the very truth. Let not the life of the world beguile you, nor let the deceiver beguile you, in regard to Allah.

(2) And if all the trees in the earth were pens, and the sea, with seven more seas to help it, (were ink), the words of Allah could not be exhausted. Lo! Allah is Mighty, Wise.

(3) Your creation and your raising (from the dead) are only as (the creation and the raising of) a single soul. Lo! Allah is Hearer, Knower.

Surah-i-Luqman

—:o:—

The likeness of those who choose other patrons than Allah is as the likeness of the spider when she taketh unto herself a house, and lo! the frailest of all houses is the spider's house, if they but knew.

We believe in that which hath been revealed unto us and revealed unto you; our God and your God is One, and unto Him we surrender.

Surah-1-Ankaboot (Spider)

—:o:—

Allah hath (now) revealed the fairest of statements, a scripture consistent, (wherein promises of reward are) paired (with threats of punishment), whereat doth creep the flesh of those who fear their Lord, so that their flesh and their hearts soften to Allah's reminder. Such is Allah's guidance wherewith He guideth whom He will. And him whom Allah sendeth astray, for him there is no guide.

Surah-i Ahzab (Troops)

—:o:—

Is not He (best) Who answereth the wronged one when

he crieth unto Him and removeth the evil, and hath made
you viceroys of the earth? Is there any God beside Allah?
Little do they reflect !

Surah-i-Naml (Ant)

—:o:—

And we (Jinns) used to sit on places (high) (in spaces)
therein to listen. But he who listened now findeth a flame
in waiting for him.

And among us there are righteous folk and among us
there are far from that. We are sects having different rules.

And we (Jinns) know not whether harm is boded unto
all who are in the earth, or whether their Lord intendeth
guidance for them.

And we know that we cannot escape from Allah in the
earth, nor can we escape by flight.

Surah-iJinn (Genii)

—:o:—

Lord of the East and West; there is no God save Him:
so choose thou Him alone for thy defender

And bear with patience what they utter, and part from
them with a fair leave-taking.

Leave Me (God) to deal with the deniers, lords of ease and comfort (in this life); and do thou respite them awhile

Surah-i-Muzammil (Shrouded)

—:o:—

And unto Midian (We sent) their brother Shu'eyb. He said: O my people! Serve Allah. Ye have no other God save Him! And give not short measure and short weight. Lo! I see you well-to-do, and lo! I fear for you the doom of a besetting Day.

O my people! Give full measure and full weight in justice, and wrong not people in respect of their goods. And do no evil in the earth, causing corruption.

Surah-i-Hud.

—:o:—

O Mankind! Eat of that which is lawful and wholesome in the earth, and follow not the footsteps of the devil Lo! he is an open enemy for you.

He enjoineth upon you only the evil and the foul, and that ye should tell concerning Allah that which ye know not.

And when it is said unto them: 'Follow that which

Allah hath revealed' they say. 'We follow that wherein we found our fathers.' What! though their fathers wholly unintelligent and had no guidance?

—:o:—

It is not righteousness that ye turn your faces to the East or to the West; but righteous is he who believeth in Allah and the Last Day and the angels and the Scripture and the Prophets; and giveth his wealth for love of Him, to kinsfolk and to orphans and the needy and the wayfarer and to those who ask, and sets slaves free; and observeth proper worship and payeth the poor-due. And those who keep their treaty when they make one, and the patient in tribulation and adversity and time of stress. Such are they who are sincere. Such are the God-fearing

—:o:—

Say (O Muslims): We believe in Allah and that which is revealed unto us and that which was revealed unto Abraham, and Ismail, and Isaac, and Jacob, and the tribes, and that which Moses and Jesus received, and that which the Prophets receive from their Lord. We make no distinction between any of them, and unto Him we have surrendered.

Surah-i-Al-Baqara

—:o:—

For those who believe not in the Hereafter is an evil similitude, and Allah's is the sublime similitude. He is the Mighty, the Wise.

If Allah were to take mankind to task for their wrong-doing, he would not leave hereon a living creature, but He repreiveth them to an appointed term, and when their term cometh they cannot put (it) off an hour nor (yet) advance (it).

Page 200

And unto Allah belongeth the Unseen of the heavens and the earth, and the matter of the Hour (of Doom) is but as a twinkling of the eye, or it is nearer still. Lo! Allah is able to do all things.

And Allah brought you forth from the wombs of your mother you knowing nothing, and gave you hearing and sight and hearts that haply ye might give thanks.

—:o:—

Page 201

(1) And (bethink you of) the day when We raise in every nation a witness against them of their own folk, and we bring thee (Muhammad) as a witness against these. And We reveal the Scripture unto thee as an exposition of All things and a guidance and a mercy and good tidings for those who have surrendered (to Allah).

(2) Lo! Allah enjoineth justice and kindness and giving to kinsfolk, and forbiddeth lewdness and abomination
and wickedness He exhorteth you in order that ye may make
heed.

(3) And purchase not a small gain at the price of Allah's
covenant Lo! that which Allah hath is better for you, if ye
did but know.

(4) That which ye have wasteth away, and that which
Allah hath remaineth.   And verily We shall pay those who
are steadfast a recompense in proportion to the best of what
they used to do.

(5) Whosoever doeth right, whether male or female, and
is a believer, him verily We shall quicken with good life, and
We shall pay them a recompense in proportion to the best
of what they used to do.

Surah-i- Nahal (Bee)

———

Thy Lord hath decreed, that ye worship none save Him,
and (that ye show) kindness to parents. If one of them or
both of them attain old age with thee, say not "Fie' unto
them nor repulse them, but speak unto them a gracious
word.

And lower unto them the wing of submission through

mercy, and say: My Lord! Have mercy on them both as they did care for me when I was little.

And they say: We will not put faith in thee (prophet) till thou cause a spring to gush forth from the earth for us,

Or thou have a garden of date-palms and grapes, and cause rivers to gush forth therein abundantly ;

Or thou cause the heaven to fall upon us piecemeal, as thou hast pretended, or bring Allah and the angels as a warrant ;

Or thou have a house of gold; or thou ascend up into heaven, and even then we will put no faith in thine ascension till thou bring down for us a book that we can read. Say (O Muhammad): My Lord be glorified! Am I naught save a mortal messenger?

Surah-i-Bani Israil (children of Israil)

—:o:—

Who made all things good which He created, and He began the creation of man from clay ;

Then He made his seed from a draught of despised fluid;

90

Then He fashioned him and breathed into him of His spirit. and appointed for you hearing and sight and hearts. Small thanks give ye!

And they say: When we are lost in the earth, how can we then be re-created? Nay but they are disbelivers in the meeting with their Lord.

Say: The angel of death, who hath charge concerning you, will gather you, and afterward unto your Lord ye will be returned.

Couldst thou but see when the guilty hang their heads before their Lord. (and say); Our Lord! We have now seen and heard, so send us back; we will do right, now we are sure.

—:o:—

Only those believe in Our revelations who, when they are reminded of them, fall down prostrate and hymn the praise of their Lord, and they are not scronful,

Who forsake their beds to cry unto their Lord and hope and spend of what We have bestowed on them.

No soul knoweth what is kept hid for them of joy, as a reward for what they used to do.
Surah-i-Sajdah (Prostration).

—:o:—

(1) Were We God then worn out by the first creation? Yet they are in doubt about a new creation.

(2) We verily created a man and We know what his soul whispereth to him, and We are nearer to him than his jugular vein.

(3) When the two Receivers receive (him) seated on the right hand and on the left.

(4) He uttereth no word but there is with him an observer ready.

(5) And the agony of death cometh in truth. (And it is said unto him): This is that which thou was wont to shun.

And the trumpet is blown. This is threatened Day.

(6) And every soul cometh, along with it a driver and a witness.

And unto the evil-doer it is said: Thou was in heedlessness of this. Now We have removed from thee thy covering, and piercing is thy sight this day.

Surah-i-Qaf. (k)

—:o:—

Allah knoweth that which every female bearth and that which the wombs absorb and that which they grow   And everything with Him is measured.

He is the Knower of the invisible and the visible, the Great, the High Exalted.

Alike of you is he who hideth the saying and he who noiseth it abroad, he who lurketh in the night and he who goeth freely in the daytime.

For him are angels ranged before him and behind him, who guard him by Allah's command. Lo! Allah changeth not the condition of a folk untill they (first) change that which is in their hearts; and if Allah willeth misfortune for a folk there is none that can repel it, nor have they a defender beside Him.

Unto Him is the real prayer. Those unto whom they pray beside Allah respond to them not at all, save as (is the response to) one who stretcheth forth his hands towards water (asking) it may come unto his mouth and it will never reach it. The prayer of disbelievers goeth (far astray.)

And unto Allah falleth prostrate whosoever is in the heavens and the earth, willingly or unwillingly, as do their shadows in the morning and the evening hours.

Surah-i Raad (Thunder).

I seek no livelihood from them, nor do I ask that they should feed Me.

Lo! Allah! He it is that giveth livelihood, the Lord of unbreakable Might.

Surah-i-(Zariat).

—:o:—

Or say they: He (prophet) hath invented it? Nay, but they will not believe!

Then let them produce speech (Quran) the like thereof, if they are truthful.

Or were they created out of naught? Or are they creators?

Or did they create the heavens and the earth? Nay, but they are sure of nothing!

Or do they own the treasures of the Lord? Or have they been given charge thereof?

Or have they any stairway (unto heaven) by means of which they overhear (decrees). Then let their listener produce some warrant manifest!

Surah-i-Toor (Mount).

Then withdraw (O Mohammad) from him who fleeth from our remembrance and desireth but the life of the world.

94

Such is their sum of knowledge. Lo! thy Lord is best aware of him who strayeth, and He is best aware of him who goeth right.

And unto Allah belongeth whatsoever is in the heavens and whatsoever is in the earth, that He may reward those who do evil with that which they have done, and reward those who do good with goodness.

Those who avoid enormities of sin and abominations, save the unwilled offences—(for them) lo! thy Lord is of vast mercy. He is best aware of you (from the time) when He created you from the earth and when ye were hidden in the bellies of your mothers. Therefore ascribe not purity unto yourselves. He is best aware of him who wardeth off evil.

Surah-i-Najm (Star).

And with Him are the keys of the invisible. None but He knoweth them. And He knoweth what is in the land and the sea, Not a leaf falleth but He knoweth it, not a grain amid the darkness of the earth, naught of wet or dry but (it is noted) in a clear record.

He it is Who gathereth you at night and knoweth that which ye commit by day. Then He raiseth you again to life therein, that the term appointed (for yon) may be accomplished. And afterward unto Him is your return. Then He will proclaim unto you what ye used to do.

He is the Omnipotent over His slaves. He sendeth guardians over you until, when death cometh unto one of you, Our messengers receive him, and they neglect not.

Then are they restored unto Allah, their Lord, the just. Surely His is the judgement. And He is the most swift of reckoners.

Surah-i-An-am (Cattle).

—:o:—

Who is guilty of more wrong than he who forgeth a lie against Allah, or saith: I am inspired, when he is not inspired in aught; and who saith: I will reveal the like of that which Allah hath revealed? If thou couldst see, when the wrongdoers reach the pangs of death and the angels stretch their hands out, saying: Deliver up your souls. This day ye are awarded doom of degradation for that ye spake concerning Allah other than the truth, and scorned His portents.

Now have ye come unto Us solitary as We did create you at the first, and ye have left behind you all that We betowed upon you, and We behold not with you those your intercessors, of whom ye claimed that they possessed a share in you. Now is the bond between you severed, and that which ye presumed hath failed you.

Surah-i-An-am (Cattle).

—:o:—

The originator of the heavens and the earth? How can He have a child, when there is for Him no consort, when He created all things and is Aware of all things ?

Such is Allah, your Lord. There is no God save Him, the Creator of all things, worship Him. And He taketh care of all things.

96

Vision comprehendeth Him not, but He comprehendeth (all) vision.   He is the Subtle, the Aware.

Proofs have come unto you from your Lord, so whoso seeth, it is for his own good and whoso is blind is blind to his own hurt.   And I (Prophet) am not a keeper over you.

Surah-i-An-am (Cattle).

—:o:—

IMPORTANCE OF THE SCIENCE OF HADITH!

The importance of the science of hadith or traditions for the understanding of the meanings of the Holy Quran and the Divine message of the Holy Prophet (peace be on him) cannot be exaggerated. The hadiths or traditions are the reports of doings and sayings of the Holy Prophet, transmitted outside the Holy Quran through a chain of known intermediaries. There are two kinds of hadith: (1) Hadith-e-Qudsi, (2) Hadithe-Nabawi. The books of hadiths constitute an important part of the Divine knowledge, which explain the Holy Quran, its fundamentals, and injunctions, and the same cannot be understood, and their details cannot be worked out properly without the aid of the Holy Prophet's explanation as contained in the books of traditions.

Dr. Iqbal, recalls to his memory the grandeur and glory of the past Muslim era, with its characteristic spiritual and cultural heritage, and gives vent to his anguish over the plight of the present Muslims of the world in his book "The Mysteries of selflessnes".

"You, who were made by God to be the Seal
Of all the peoples dwelling upon earth,
That all beginnings might in you find end;
Whose saints were prophet like, whose wounded
    hearts
Wove into unity the souls of men ;
Why are you fallen now so far astray

From Mecca's holy Kaaba, all bemused
By the strange beauty of the Christian's way?
The very skies are but a gathering
Of your Street's dust, yourselves the cynosure
Of all men's eyes; whither in restless haste
Do you now hurry like a storm-tossed wave.
What new diversion seeking.

According to Dr. Iqbal, the Muslims have gone down into abyss of darkness because the individual self has failed to identify and merge itself with the self of the community and the latter has forsaken the divine law, and lost the power to resist evil collectively or individually. The example and the precept of the Holy Prophet (peace be on him) has been ignored on the plea of expediency; and that faith is not supported by actions or deeds. In short, the down-fall of the Millat has been brought about to a large extent by several factors, the chief of which, is that with the impact of the western civilization, and its dazzling ascendancy in the political and material spheres, the science of traditions and the brilliant example of the Holy Prophet (peace be on him), has been thrown into the background.

Our heart, therefore, bleeds when we ponder over the grave loss caused by the new and old theologians and men expert in the science of traditions to the divine knowledge, that was once incorporated in the recorded literature of hadiths ascribeable to the Holy Prophet (peace be on him) and to his companions. How this process was brought about, we are discussing the same in the following lines. Let us refer to Bukhari Shariff the famous book of traditions. There is an acknowledgement on the part of its author that after sifting, checking, and thorough examination of the hadith and traditions, he selected five thousand authentic traditions, out of a vast sea of literature comprising one million traditions, available in his time. There is also an acknowledgement on the part of this great intellectual that he himself knew by heart at least one lakh traditions but since they lacked authenticity and validity, he made a selection of a small part from this field of literature.

The Holy Prophet used to receive Divine revelation un-interruptedly throughout his life as an apostle of God for a period of 23 years; he in his turn confided the same to his close associates and his companions, he knew through his divine knowledge the past historical events and the future events to take place in this world. Surah-i-Rome and Surah-i-Asra (Night Journey), adequately testify to this fact, Not only this but the Holy Quran contains references to general sciences, the basic facts about the origin of the universe, and the origin of the biological life, which are under investigation in the present times. The miracle of life is still a mystery which the human mind has failed to uncover. The Holy Quran has references, therefore, to profound scientific and spiritual truths. It is impossible to believe that the fundamentals and other verities that we come across in the Holy Quran, the Holy Prophet (peace be on him) must have left the same unexplained. The commentators of the Holy Quran are silent, or if they explain a thing on the subject of scientific truths, they do it unsatisfactorily and are unable to explain the specific verses relating to the origin of the universe, the origin of life, the formation of the solar system, the future shape of the things to come about. The Holy Prophet (peace be on him), we presume, must have explained these fundamentals; but when the science of traditions developed in the third century Hijri, the traditions explaining the scientific truths were rejected or thrown aside on the ground that the same were beyond the intellectual comprehension of an average person.

It must, however, be mentioned that the companions of the Holy Prophet (peace be on Him), namely, Hazrat Abu Hurera, Abdullah Bin Masud, Zed Bin Sabit and Anas Bin Malik, and a host of other pious souls were always with the Holy Prophet (peace be on him), watching, listening and even recording the doings and sayings of the Holy Prophet (peace be on him) Hazrat Abu Hurera, notably knew at least five thousand hadiths, (5000), while Ummi Aisha is reported to have known by heart about three thousand sayings of the Holy Prophet (peace be on him). But the tratvaditionists and theologians recorded this divine knowledge in their books to the extent of five or six per cent out of a vast sea of literature available in their times in the third century of Islam. Had the vast divine knowledge survived to this day the onslaught of the times, the Muslims would not have entered the dark ages, nor the scientific knowledge about the cosmos, the mysteries of life and miracles would have remained uncovered. It must be noted that the process of selection and rejection, and screening of the traditions was based upon certain rules and principles. For instance, a tradition was regarded as weak and unauthentic if the reporter, or the narrator was of a weak memory, or of a doubtful character, or whose source of knowledge was doubtful and unreliable, or if the subject matter of the hadith under investigation was beyond the intellect of an average human, or the hadiths conferred disproportionate reward or punishment for petty acts of commission or ommission. In short, these rules and principles employed in the process of selection and rejection were responsible for the obliteration of a considerable size of the divine knowledge, specially the knowledge relating to the general sciences.

Truly speaking, the meanings and interpretations of the Holy Quran is dependent largely upon the divine knowledge, recorded and incorporated in traditions, and the same also explain any ambiguity in the understanding of the doctrinal truth of the same When we read the Holy Quran, we find all kinds of commentaries in abundance which facilitate the understanding of the meanings and import of the Holy Book; but when we come across certain specific verses relating to scientific truth about the origin of the universe, or the origin of the organic life or the biological evolution of man or when we come across philosophical truth about the origin of the soul or its final return, we find commentaries silent and explanations, if any, unsatisfactory and quite inadequate for our purpose.

It is a matter of regret that the modern westernised mind even rejects this meagre divine knowledge available to us in the present day world on the ground of its being fossilised, desultory, or out of tune with the modern times. In doing so they in fact attack the very base of the Holy Quran. The results have been that we have been cut off from the divine moornings and from the spiritual womb of the traditions. It is noteworthy that we lack the necessary illumination and knowledge to interpret and understand correctly several verses of the Holy Quran for want of authentic and reliable knowledge of the hadiths but there are also traditions which are authentic, and these need not be rejected.

102

To the modern critic of the science of hadith, our plea is to study the whole Quran as it deserves to be studied and to find for himself how important are the traditions in the understanding of the commandments of the Holy Quran regarding the various institutions of Salat (prayers) Zakat (tax) Haj (Pilgrimage to Macca) Jehad (Holy Wars), and the conception of God and in working out the details of the Quranic injunctions. Any thing in the tradition that goes against the basic teaching of the Holy Quran can be termed as concocted and false, and then weaned out. We, therefore, deprecate the tendency on the part of critics to under-value or to belittle the importance of the science of hadiths, Nevertheless, the Holy Quran, it must be admitted contains numerous verses which are self explanatory, and its meanings are v y clear when read in their true context.

The Holy Quran is a divine revelation, preserved and protected for mankind by the divine powers themselves. It contains eternal truths and fundamentals which it tries to reassert, rediscover, and rearrange in order to bring into focus again the central truths, which have suffered temporary eclipse. The Quranic doctrines have dynamism and practicability and are so constituted as to conform to the human nature and its basic requirements. The Holy Quran and the science of hadith, therefore, constitute a corrective measure for all the imbalances in the spiritual, material and social values.

Surah-i-Asra (Night Journrey), bears ample testimony to the fact that the Holy Prophet (peace be on him) during the ascension into the unknown space came across a number of heavenly objects, scenes of ecstasic beauties, and paradisial visions. Not only this but the Holy Prophet (peace be on him) saw the worst plight of the hardened criminals and enemies of God and men in the hell-fire. The Holy Prophet possessed spiritual eyes through which he saw all these as if in a divine television mirror, alongwith it he knew through divine knowledge the historial events belonging to the remote past, present, and also the future events to take place. In short he foresaw and visualised what the ultimate human destiny is going to be. We again take the liberty to quote Dr. Iqbal, regarding the divine light possessed by the Holy Prophet (peace be on him).

In this world
Thou lit the lamp of life, as thou didst teach
God's servitors a godly mastery.
Without thee, whatsoever form indwelt
This habitat of water and of clay
Was put to shame in utter bankruptcy;
Till, when thy breath drew fire from the cold dust
And Adam made of Earth's dead particles,
Each Atom caught the skirts of Sun and moon.

Allama Yusuf Ali, in his book "The Message of Islam" (page 50), has written about the Holy Prophet (peace be on him).

"But Muhammad came in the fullest blaze of history;

With no learning he put to shame the wisdom of learned;

In hills and valleys, caves and deserts, he wandered, but never lost his way of truth and righteousness;

From his pure and spotless hearts the Angels washed off the dust that flew around him;

Through the way of crooked city folk, he walked upright and straight.

And won from them the ungrudging name of the Man of Faith who never broke his word.

To the Praiseworthy indeed be praise:

Born in the Sacred City, he destroyed its superstitions;

Loyal to his people to the core, he stood for all humanity ;

Orphan-born and poor, he envied not the rich, and made his special care all those whom the world neglected or oppressed,

Orphans, women, slaves, and those in need of food or comforts, mental solace, spiritual strength, or virtues down-trodden in the haunts of men."

Hence divine knowledge, embodied in the traditions cannot be under-valued or rejected for the Holy Quran says "He (Holy Prophet) does not speak out of his personal desire (or motive) but his wise utterances are due to divine inspirations". (Surah-i-Najm). Let us look into the reasons for this poor Divine knowledge recorded in traditions.

In the beginning of the third century Hijri a group of

people, known as Ulma-i-Su (misguided and self appointed jurists and theologians), grew up who put on the garb of erudition, began to corrupt and concoct traditions and hadiths and put the same before the simple Muslims for acceptance, alleging that these were authentic and supported by the Holy Prophet and his companions. They did so in order to please the monarchical dictators, who wanted to propagate their false and perverted theories of politics, economy, and religion. It must be noted that after the martyrdom of Hazrat Hussain (peace be on him), the Islamic institutions lost their pristine beauty. These latter institutions were based upon monarchy, dictatorship, or feudualism, which promoted irreligiousness and consequently immorality in the Islamic Polity.

Thus being afraid of the current counterfeit and concoction in their times, the great intellectuals and leaders of men like Imam Malik, Muslim and Imam Bukhari devised some principles and methods by which they undertook the task to classify Hadith into (1) authentic and unauthentic (2) reliable and unreliable, and into several classes. In this manner while making a judicious selection or rejection, or weaning the true from the false they, it appears, unintentionally did away with a greater part of traditions specially belonging to general sciences.

We cannot understand and interpret the Holy Quran without reference to the traditions which are the part and parcel of the divine knowledge, bequeathed to us by our messenger of Allah. The Holy Quran revives, reiterates and re-defines the eternal truths and verities already embodied in the ancient scriptures like the Gospel, Torat, and other scriptures belonging to the Semitic religion. It attempts to reconstruct basic doctrines within the frame work of old scriptural truths. The Holy Quran declares the Unity of God "There is no god, but the God and Mohammed (peace be on him), the seal of all the apostles of God". Besides. the Holy Quran delivers the message of a World ideology of "one God, one humanity, and one world, resurrection and accountability of man before his Creator and Universal brotherhood of man and a message of true faith, prayers and actions" Those who subscribe to the Quranic ideology, which the Holy Quran presents, constitute an ideal and universal brotherhood of men believing in the Unity of God and in his promise for a good life in this world and in the hereafter.

It must be be said to the credit of our pious Imams, that they took great pains in their great efforts in consolidating the science of hadith, in drawing a demarcation line between the false and the true, and warned the future theologians from the danger of concoction and counterfeit—(see Fahme-Quran in Urdu by Molvi Saeed Ahmed, M.A). It must be added that the criterion for judging whether a Hadith is false or concocted or partly concocted is to see whether the Hadith under reference contradicts the Quranic teaching or whether it is against equity, justice, fairplay, and morality, or against the universal sense of justice, or whether it recommends monasticism or monkish life. So it is the function of the present day theologians to make a distinction between the true and the false.

EXTRACTS FROM THE SPEECHES OF THE HOLY PROPHET

—:o:—

We give here-under some extracts from the speeches of the holy Prophet (peace be on him), who delivered them from time to time on important occasions. From these one can see that all the feelings, thoughts and actions of the Holy Messenger of God were directed towards the good of the whole world, and to the universal religion he practised during his entire life.

—:o:—

The glittering gems of wisdom

"Well, verily the most veracious discourse is the Book of Allah. The most trustworthy handle-hold is the word of piety.

The best of the religions is the religion of Ibrahim, (*i.e.* Islam). The best of the precedent is the precedent of Muhammed.

The noblest speech is the invocation of Allah. The finest of the narratives is this Quran.

The best of the affairs is that which have been firmly resolved upon. The worst things in religion are the newly created ones. The best of the ways is the ways of the Prophets. The noblest death is the death of martyrs.

The greatest blindness is going astray after guidance.
The best of the actions is that which benefits. The best
guidance is that which is followed (in practice). The worst
blindness is the blindness of the heart. The upper hand is
better than the lower hand. The little but sufficient is better
than abundant but alluring. The worst apology is that which
is made at the point of death. The worst regret is that which
will be felt on the Day of Resurrection.

One of (the sources of) the greatest sins is the false
tongue. The best richness is the richness of the soul. The
best provision is piety. The highest philosophy is the fear of
Allah, the Mighty and the Great. The best thing to be
respected in the hearts is firm belief and the doubt is
infidelity.

Wailing is an act of ignorance. The (bad) poetry comes
from devil. Wine is the centre of crimes. The worst food is
the property of the orphan. Blessed is he who receives
admonition from others.

Each one of you must resort to a place of four cubits
(grave). The pivot of action is its ends. The worst dream
is false dream. Whatever is to come is near. To abuse a
believer is transgression and the fight against him is infidelity.
To backbite him is a disobedience to Allah. Inviolability
(and sacredness) of his property is like that of his blood (life).

"One who swears by Allah (falsely), He falsifies him. He
who pardons (others), He pardons him. He who blots out
(others' sins), Allah blots out his sins.

He who represses the anger Allah rewards him. He who
persevers in a misfortune, Allah indemnifies him.

He who pursues renown (*i.e.* acts only for the sake of
advertisement and being heard), Allah disgraces him. He
who has patience, Allah gives him double. He who disobeys
Allah, Allah chastises him.

I beg pardon from Allah. I beg pardon from Allah. I
beg pardon from Allah.'' Extract of the speech delivered
on the field of the battle at Tabuk.

—:o:—

'O tribe of the Quraish. verily Allah removed from you
the pride of the age of ignorance and its ancestral vainglory
Men are the progeny of Adam and Adam came out of earth.'
Then the Holy Prophet recited this verse ; O mankind, We
have created you out of a male and a female; and We have
divided you into nations and tribes; so that you may recognise
one another. Verily the more honourable among you to
Allah is he who is more pious. Indeed, Allah is All-knowing
and Omniscient.

'O tribe of Quraish, what behaviour do you expect from
me? They said: (We expect) good: you are a noble brother
and the son of a noble brother.'

He said: I say to you what Joseph said to his brothers:
"No reproach is upon you today; may Allah forgive you and
He is the most compassionate of the compassionates. Go
away; you ore free."

110

Extract of the speech delivered on the (victory) of Mecca!

—:o:—

Lo, I have, indeed, been given the keys of the treasures of the earth. By Allah I do not fear for you that you will turn polytheists after me. But I fear you that you will be entangled in them, then will fight one another and will perish like those who perished before you.

"O people, verily the sins spoil the blessings and change the lots. When the people are good, their rulers do good to them and when the people are bad, they opress them."

Then he said: "There may be some rights which I owe to you and I am nothing but a human being. So if there be any man whose honour I have injured a bit, there is my honour; he may retaliate.

Whosoever he may be, if I have wounded a bit of his skin, here is my skin; He may retaliate.

"Whosoever he may be, if I have taken anything from his property so he may take. Know that he, among you, is more loyal to me who has got such a thing takes it or absolves me: then I meet my Lord while I am absolved.

Nobody should say, I fear enmity and grudge of the Apostle of Allah. Verily these things are not in my nature and character. He whose passion has overcome him in aught, should seek help from me so that I may pray for him. (Exract from the speech delivered by the H. Prophet five days before his death. The above are the excerpt from 'The Orations' of Mohammed by Maulana Mohd. Ubaidul Akbar).

**The principles of life of the Holy Prophet can be
known from a famous tradition mentioned
by Hafiz Ghulam Sarwar! in his book
"Muhammed the Holy Prophet"!**

—:o:—

"Ali Bin Abu Talib once asked the Prophet as to what
was his Sunnah. This is what Muhammad (peace be on
him) said:

> Knowledge of God is my Capital;
> Reason is the root of my Faith;
> Love is my Foundation;
> Enthusiasm is my Horse;
> Remembrance of God is my Friend;
> Firmness is my Treasure;
> Sorrow is my Companion;
> Science is my Weapon;
> Patience is my Mantle;
> Contentment is my Booty;
> Poverty is my Pride;
> Devotion is my Art;
> Conviction is my Power;
> Truth is my Redeemer;
> Obedience is my Sufficiency;
> Struggle is my Manner; and
> My Plearure is in my Prayer.

SOME IMPORTANT AND WELL KNOWN SAYINGS OF THE HOLY PROPHET ARE GIVEN HEREUNDER!

Verily is destroyed the people before you that when a
noble man among them commited a theft, they let him off,

and when a weak man committed theft from among them they executed sentence on him.

By Him in whose hand is the soul of Muhammad, had Fatimah, the daughter of Muhammad, committed a theft, I would have cut off her hand.

DIGNITY OF LABOUR!

Pray to God morning and evening, and spend the day in thy pursuits.

He who worketh neither for himself, nor for others shall not recieve the reward of God.

Whoso is able and fit, yet worketh not for himself nor for others, God is not kind to him.

O God, keep me from inability and laziness.

Those who earn an honest living are the beloved of God.

God is gracious to him that earneth his living by his own labour and not by begging.

Pay the workman his wages before his perspiration is dried up.

Whoever monopolises trade is a transgressor.

Whosoever buyeth and selleth at a cheap rate gaineth great advantage, and he that purchaseth and hoardeth to sell at a high rate incurreth God's displeasure.

113

WOMEN!

Women are the twin-halves of men.

When a women observeth the five time of prayer, and fasteth during the month of Ramzan, and is chaste, and is not disobedient to her hushand, then tell her to enter Paradise by whichever door she pleaseth.

He is the best of Muslims whose disposition is best: and best of you are they who behave best to their wives.

The thing which is lawful, but disliked by God, is divorce.

MUSLIM!

A Muslim is he from whose tongue and hands Muslims are safe; and a Muhajir (emigrant through persecution, or to help the good cause) is he who fleeth from what God has forbidden.

He is not a perfect Muslim who eateth his fill and leaveth his neighbours hungry.

Whoso believeth in one God and the life beyond, let him not Injure his neighbours.

ASCETICISM!

Monasticism is not countenanced by Islam.

To commit suicide is one of the mortal crimes.

Wish not death before its time comes.

A Muslim who mixes with others and shares their burdens is better then one who lives a life of seclusion and contemplation.

PRAYERS !

The Lord regardeth not a prayer in which the heart doth not accompany the body.

He whom prayer preventeth not from wrongdoing and evil increaseth in naught save in remoteness from the Lord.

Adore God as you would if you saw Him; for, if you see Him not He seeth you.

Prayer brings the Faithful into communion with his Cherisher.

KITHAND KIN !

The blessings of Allah do not descend upon the family in which is one who deserteth his relations.

He who wisheth to enter Paradise must please his father and mother.

The duty of a younger to an elder brother is as that of a child to its father.

Whosover is kind to the creation, God is kind to him.

REASON AND COMMON SENSE!

The first thing created was Reason.

God hath not created anything better than Reason, or anything more perfect or more beautiful than Reason. The benefits which Allah giveth are on its account, and understanding is by it; and Allah's displeasure is caused by it, and by it are rewards and punishments.

Verily a man hath performed prayers, fasts, charity, pilgrimage, and all other good deeds; but he will not be rewarded but in proportion to the sense he employeth.

ENVY AND SUSPICION !

Envy and suspicion disintegrate society.

Suspicion is the blackest lie.

Keep yourselves far from envy, for it eateth up and taketh away good actions, like as fire eateth up and burneth wood.

PRAYER !

Say your prayers standing; but if you are not able, do it sitting; and if not sitting, in bed.

He whom prayer preventh not from wrong-doing and evil, increaseth in naught save in remoteness from the Lord.

PARADISE !

Guard yourselves from six things, and I am your security for Paradise: When you speak, speak the truth; perform when you promise; discharge your trust; be chaste in thought and action; and withhold your hand from striking, from taking that which is unlawful and bad.

EDUCATION !

He dieth not who taketh to learning.

The ink of the scholar is more holy than the blood of the martyr.

He who leaveth home in search of knowledge walketh in the path of Allah.

The acquisition of knowledge is a duty incumbent on every Muslim, male and female.

Acquire knowledge. It enableth the possessor to distinguish right from wrong; it lighteth the way to heaven; it is our friend in the desert, our society in solitude, our companion when friendless; it guideth us to happiness; it sustains us in misery; it is an ornament among friends and an armonr against enemies.

Seek after knowledge though it be in China.

PRAYER!

O Lord! unite our hearts, improve our natural relation ship; show us the path of peace; protect us against lewdness whether open or secret, bless our ears, eyes, and hearts; and families. O Lord! forgive us our sins for thou art the most Gracious and Forgiving.

—:o:—

The Cosmic Hazards of the planet earth.

—:o:—

The sciences of astronomy and space have made tremendous advances in the sphere of knowledge. The astronomers and cosmologists have discovered billions and trillions of stars, planets and their satellites. There are thousands of galaxies floating in the vast interstellar space with the speed even of light. The rule is-far away the galaxy the faster is its speed.

The American Astronauts by achieving lunar walks on the moon have proved beyond doubts that our planet earth is nothing but a spacecraft, moving in the interstellar space precariously with a speed of 67000 miles per hour. Our planet earth is moving and spinning round the sun in an orderly manner in accordance with the divine schemes since its mysterious birth from times unknown. It is spinning towards its divinely destined goal.

The vast expanding universe in which we live had a mysterious beginning and it must have an abrupt end at a time known to the divine powers themselves. The sun, the moon, and all the things and all the varied natural forces found in our universe are subservient to man, the crown of the creation and the king pin of the un verse All that lie in the heavens and in the earth belong to Allah. He created man to be free to worship God, to govern, and to derive maximum advantage from the created things. The treasures of the earth and all its natural wealth, its flowers and fauna are the blessings of Allah. The book of Allah has taught us.

1. To God we belong and to Him is our ultimate return.

2. Adam was created from dust and humanity is one and indivisib e

3, Human life does not end on this planet earth but it continnes and the Human soul soars higher and higher to reach its divine goal in the Hereafter and humans are responsible before the Supreme Judge for their deeds good or bad

4. The secrets of the cosmos and of the earrh belong to Allah and in the words of the Holy Quran the disintegration of the entire universe is but a matter of seconds.

Despite our big advances in the field of scientific know how and b:eakthrough in the sphere of the comprehensive sciences, we have failed to susiain human values. On the contrary we stand to day disillusioned when we witness international conspiracies to malign true religion and to stifle the truth.

The Holy Quran pin points the fact about numerous hazards and dangers to which our planet earth is constantly exposed at every moment. Not only this but our modern sciences of astronomy and cosmology have also spelled out disintegration of our globe with a bang. Science has discovered for us that our sun is 884000 miles in Diameter, and consuming about 584 millions tons of hydrogen per second to maintain its thermo nuclear activity in its core in order to supply life giving heat to its satellites. Science has discoverd for us that the death rays or the gamma rays from the furnace of the sun's core is shielded by an elastic and moving shell the thickness of which is about 80,000 miles. The suns' gamma rays and its ultra voilet rays have to pass through photo sphere, the chromo and the corona spheres. In order to reach our earth, while doing so these rays are converted to life-giving heat, a b essing from our Lord.

If the sun begins to rain or shower death rays direct upon us—in this case, our earth shall be reduced to a mere cinder or to a heap of ashes or to a mcre mass of gases. Then the question arises. Do we humans possess any other protective sheild or any alternate shell of mass of gases besides the God-given protective shell over the furnace of the sun or any alternate protecting magnetic sphere which the Sciences have also discovered for us (and which surrounds the earth itself. The flames and flares of the furnace of the sun, it must be said, are so terrific that they shoot up to about one million miles.

Science has recorded for us that there are about 100000 small and big asteriods-islands and rocky mountains, hovering and orbiting between the sphere of the Mars and the Jupitor. These floating islands and mountains have been identified and named. One of the huge asteriod, namely Ceres is 480 miles in diametre and measuring about 7 Lakh square miles in area. The asteriod Pallas is three hundred miles in diametre. Then there is the Vesta 240 miles in Diametre, Erose, Icarious and Hermes and a host of others. Then there are the Trojans orbiting in the front and behind the planet Jupitor, which is I300, times bigger than our planet earth. Our sky overhead, therefore, is dotted with numerous but dangerious asteriods and Comets. These mysterious rocky asteriods are encircling and orbiting round the sun day and night, and these some-times come very close to our earth itself. Science has recorded for us that there are some Star wounds-signs of the fall of the asteriods and comets on the surface of our earth. One of the star wounds has been found in Arizona and another in Australia. But these star wounds over the surface of our earth are very old.

These asteriods and comets posses the potentiality to undo the planet earth within seconds. But Allah out of His mercy is protecting us from all the cosmic hazards, and on the contrary, the blows from the cosmos have constantly been borne out by the other planets like the Mars, the venus, and the Jup tor and specially by our moon itself. This is the reason why the surface of these planets have scars and craters. Our powerful cameras are a witness to this intrinsic truth.

It must be mentioned that there are one lakh comets as well orbiting round the sun. Their orbital flight is typical, and in 1908, the tail of a comet struck soveit Russia causing havoc in the region of Siberia, where nume-rous kind of meteorites were pickwd up. The science of cosmology has pointed out numerons dangers to which our planet earth is exposed. Our earth in its elliptical flight does several critical functions of whobbling, nodding and jumping and in doing so it never loses its balance and its angular momentum on its axis round the sun is very mysterious.

The holy Quran in its chapter, namely Aaraf records that in the times of Moses a mutititude of peoples gathering was scared away when a rocky mountain appeared very close on the head of the unbeleiving crowd. The Holy Quran also records that the peoples belonging to the prophet Lut (Peace be upon him) were destroyed by the Cosmic rocks and their dewellings levelled down because these people were sexually mad and were homo-sexuals. The Holy Quran in its Chapter namely, Qiamat-resurrection predicts the end of the cosmos including the earth itself on the occurrence of a specific cosmic phenomena.

The holy book of Allah says in Sura-i-Qiamat (Resurrection), people ask about the ressuurection day. Say 0 Prophet 'When the eyes will be blinded (due to the excessive dazzling), and the moon eclipsed, and the sun, and the moon coming closer to each other: (at that) hour men will cry "where is the shelter but there will be no shelter except that of Allah's"-

This specific cosmic natural phenomena, pin pointed by the Holy Quran has to be interpreted and understood in the light of the modern sciences and in the light of the Holy Prophet"s prediction, namely, that at the time of the resurrection the sun will rise from the west instead of the east. The implications of this prediction are that either the earth will comence a reverse course of journey from the east towards the west and in doing so it will change its angular momentum, or that the planet earth will go higher towards the sun by at least 90 lakhs of miles towards the sun. The moon which is captive of the earth will get itself burnt out and also get itself completely burst. The earth itself reduced: to the original primordial gases due the excessive heat of the sun.

God knows better what are the real implications of the Quranic preditions of the cosmic phenomena about the prophesied final eclipse of the moon, heralding the end of the entire cosmos.

The question arises can the modern sciences of astronomy foresee the disintegration of the entire existing universe and point out any solution and avert the impending doom of the material world in which we live.

In fact our modern sciences are incapable even to locate any cosmic trouble that is going to afflict our planet earth in the future. The Quranic prophecy about the doom and abrupt end of the cosmos is inevitable, but the hour of the doom of the same is hidden in the womb of the future. The men of sciences, with a few exceptions, in the present times have gone astray because they scruplously avoid even to mention the name of God in their writings, and they do not even discern any divinity in the created things. On the contrary, the men of sciences believe in the blind mechanical chance about the cosmos, which according to them came into existance with a sudden explosion and that the whole wisely-visioned order found in the universe is not the work of a Divine Creator. These men of sciences are abetted in this belief by the Godlessness of the communistic world. It may, however, he mentioned that there occured in the

U.S.A. on the 7th March 1970 a partial eclipse of the sun, causing darknes in the midday due to the fact that our moon had gone 12000 thousands of miles nearer to the earth in its orbital flight causing a partial eclipse for three minutes. Consequently there was darkness in the midday over a path of 100 miles in some parts of the pacific and in the U S A. This eclipse of the sun has tremendous significance for us, because our earth itself prior to its abrupt end will have to follow a similar major cosmic phenomena of the eclipse of the moon as predictd in the holy book of Allah. This eclipse of the moon will be the first and the last, heralding the doom of the entire cosmos, and will be dumb-founding the living cosmologists of the world.

The holy prophet of Islam has very faithfully conveyed to the world a divine message about the present universe in which we live and about other stable universes and planets like the present one But these universes have not been located as yet by the present astronomers despite their sophisticated electronic devices and antannas. In sura-i-Talaq the holy Quran has recorded some 1400 year's back that 'He (God) created seven universes and such other planets like the existing planet earth where Allah's sovereignty also extends to The chapter known as sura-Rahman declares that there are in existence several rich lands full of gardens meant for righteous people in the heavens besides the present unstable universe, and this sura repeats a question 31 times" "Which of the bounties of thy Lord will ye and ye (the humans and the Jinns) deny."?

So it is the sacred task of the future scientists and
astronomers to discover and locate the new universes inden-
tified by the holy Quran and the Holy prophet of Islam,
whose great personality as an eminent cosmologist will be
unfolded with the passing of the times.

—: o: —

BIBLIOGRAPHY

(1) Sufism, by A. J. Arberry.

(2) Man and His Universe, by John Langdon Davies.

(3) Universe of Science, by Professor Levy.

(4) One Hundred Most Important People, Life of Caspersson, by Donald Robinson.

(5) Holy Quran, by Allama Yousuf Ali.

(6) The Koran Interpreted by Professor A.J. Arberry.

(7) The Glorious Quran, by Mohd. Pikhthall.

(8) Holy Quran, by Palmer.

(9) Lugatul Quran, by Maulana Syed Abdul Daim Jalali.

(10) Holy Quran, by Shah Abdul Aziz.

(11) Fahme Quran (In Urdu), by Molvi Mohd. Saeed.

(12) The Islamic Ideology, by Dr. Khalifa Abdul Hakim.

(13) The Metaphysics of Maulana Roomi by Dr. Khalifa Abdul Hakim.

(14) The Ideology of the Future, by Dr. M. Rafiuddin

(15) The Metaphysics of Dr. Iqbal, by Dr. Ishrat Husein.

(16) Reconstruction of Religious Thought, by Dr. Iqbal.

(17) The Message of Islam, by A. Yusuf Ali.

(18) Mysteries of Selflessness, by Dr. Iqbal, translated by Prof. A. J. Arberry.

(19) Sufi Message, by Inayat Khan.

(20) An Introduction to Soofy Doctrine, by Titus Burckhardt. translated by D.M. Matheson.

(21) The Faith and Practice of Al Ghazali, by W. Montgomery Watt.

(22) The Quintessence of Islam, by Ashfaque Hussain.

(23) Ahya-ul-Ulum In Urdu), by Imam Ghazali

(24) Islamic Occasionalism And Its Critique, by Aberroes and Aquina! by Majeed Fakhry.

(25) Support of The Faith, Orientalia Publication, by Molvi Ismail (Shaheed)

(26) The Philosophy of the Holy Quran by Hafiz Ghulam Sarwar.

(27) Quran and Ilme Jadid (in Urdu), by Dr. M. Rafi Uddin.

(28) (1) Door of Perception (2) Hell and Heaven, by Aldous Huxley.

(29) Mohammed (The Prophet of Islam), by Hafiz Ghulam Sarwar.

(30) The Orations of Mohammed, by Maulana Ubedul Akbar.